Reclaiming Food Securit

In this challenging work, the author argues that the goal of any food system should not simply be to provide the cheapest calories possible. A secure food system is one that affords people and nations—in both the present and the future—the capabilities to prosper and lead long, happy, and healthy lives. For a variety of reasons, food security has come to be synonymous with cheap calorie security. On this measure, the last fifty years have been a remarkable success.

But the author shows that these cheap calories have also come at great cost—to the environment, individual and societal well-being, human health, and the food sovereignty of nations. The book begins by reviewing the concept of food security, particularly as it has been enacted within agrifood and international policy over the last century. After proposing a coherent definition, the author then assesses empirically whether these policies have actually made us and the environment any better off. One of the many ways the author accomplishes this task is by introducing the Food and Human Security Index (FHSI) in an original attempt to improve measurement and quantification of the affording qualities of food systems. An FHSI score is calculated for 126 countries based on indicators of objective and subjective well-being, nutrition, ecological sustainability, food dependency, and food system market concentration. The final FHSI ranking produces many counter-intuitive results. Why, for example, does Costa Rica top the ranking, while the United States comes in at number 55?

The author concludes by arguing for the need to reclaim food security by returning the concept to something akin to its original spirit, identified earlier in the book. While starting at the level of the farm, the concluding chapter focuses most of its attention beyond the farm gate, recognizing that food security is about more than just issues surrounding production. For example, space is made in this chapter to address the important question of "What can we eat if not GDP?" We need, the author contends, a thoroughly sociological rendering of food security: a position that views food security not as a thing—or an end in itself—but as a process that ought to make people and the planet better off.

Michael Carolan is a Professor at Colorado State University, USA, and Chair of its Department of Sociology. Some of his recent books include *The Real Cost of Cheap Food* (Routledge), *The Sociology of Food and Agriculture* (Routledge), and *Society and the Environment: Pragmatic Solutions to Ecological Issues* (Westview Press).

"Never again should we use the phrase 'food security' – in the classroom, in the literature, or at the dinner table – without invoking Carolan's meaning in his aptly titled *Reclaiming Food Security*, not just simply meeting calorie needs but fostering well-being in current and future generations." — *Christine M. Porter, Assistant Professor of Public Health and Food Dignity Project Director, University of Wyoming, USA*

"Carolan challenges the prevailing assumptions about food security and, in so doing, recovers the true spirit of the term by reconnecting it to human welfare. Rich in detail, broad in scope, and thoroughly engaging to read. Genuinely refreshing scholarship" — *Colin Sage, University College Cork, Republic of Ireland*

"A brilliant, bold and path-breaking intervention into world food politics. This easy-to-read book changes how we must think about and work on food security. The conceptual and analytic tool of the Food and Human Security Index compellingly brings social sense back into the food security debate. A powerful, empirically grounded, thought experiment directed at enacting different human and food futures." — *Richard Le Heron, University of Auckland, New Zealand*

Books in the Earthscan Food and Agriculture Series

Reclaiming Food Security

Michael Carolan

LONDON AND NEW YORK

First published 2013
by Routledge
2 Park Square, Milton Park, Abingdon, Oxon, OX14 4RN

Simultaneously published in the USA and Canada
by Routledge
711 Third Avenue, New York, NY 10017

Routledge is an imprint of the Taylor & Francis Group, an informa business

British Library Cataloguing in Publication Data
A catalogue record for this book is available from the British Library

Library of Congress Cataloging-in-Publication Data
Carolan, Michael S.
  Reclaiming food security / Michael S. Carolan. — 1st ed.
    p. cm.
Includes bibliographical references and index.
  1. Food security—Social aspects.   2. Human security.
  3. Agriculture—Environmental aspects.   I. Title.
  HD9000.5.C2583 2013
  338.1'9—dc23

                                        2012037495

ISBN: 978-0-415-81695-3 (hbk)
ISBN: 978-0-415-81696-0 (pbk)
ISBN: 978-0-203-38793-1 (ebk)

Typeset in Sabon
by RefineCatch Limited, Bungay, Suffolk

Contents

Figures

Tables

Boxes

Acknowledgements

This book was a lot of fun to write. Reviewing endless data sets and constructing hundreds of scatterplots; historically tracing food security's emergence and transformation; and trying to devise some sort of food and human security indicator: it all made for an exciting journey. I also took great pleasure drawing insights, inspiration, and support from a brilliant cast of supporting characters: Hugh Campbell, Geoff Lawrence, Richard Le Heron, Nick Lewis, Phil McMichael, Mara Miele, Chris Rosin, and Paul Stock. I am extremely grateful to you all. Thanks also to Tim Hardwick for seeing the value of this project, even during its early formative stages.

There are many additional people I would like to thank, if only I knew your names. I am talking not only about the reviewers of the book proposal and final manuscript, though I am truly thankful for your comments and appreciative of the time commitments tied to the process. Chapter 6 of this book—where the Food and Human Security Index is introduced—has been twice peer-reviewed, as it appeared earlier, in a slightly altered form, in a special issue on food security (2012, volume 19, issue 2) of the *International Journal of Sociology of Agriculture and Food*. My thanks therefore also go out to the reviewers of that article.

Yet my largest debt is to Nora. You not only helped me find the time to write but made it possible for me to take those trips (to as far away as New Zealand) that allowed me to be in immediate contact with many of the names mentioned above. Thank you, Nora. Thank you, one and all.

Chapter 1

Introduction

A quick Google search of the term "food security" (in quotes to ensure an accurate count) yields a staggering 19.7 million "hits", more than "malnutrition" (17.6 million), "sustainable agriculture" (5.9 million), "green revolution" (5 million), and "food sovereignty" (0.791 million). And the term's already-high visibility looks to be only increasing. When updating these search figures, from May 2012 to July 2012, food security's hits had increased by more than one million while, for example, food sovereignty's had decreased by roughly 100,000. Not that I am surprised by any of this. My experiences with agriculture professionals, policy-makers, students (I am a professor at Colorado State University), and the general public have yielded similar results. While the term "food security" is less than forty years old—it was first used in a policy context at the 1974 World Food Congress—its diffusion through society has been rapid and thorough. Having become such a part of collective discourse, I frequently call upon the term when describing what I do, particularly when meeting someone for the first time. Not surprisingly, the moniker "sociologist interested in issues related to food, agriculture, and the environment" is often met with hollow looks. Identifying what I do with food security, conversely, triggers not only understanding but a good deal of thoughtful conversation, too.

Literally hundreds of definitions of food security are scattered throughout the literature—a review from over twenty years ago, the last of its kind to be conducted, yielded almost two hundred (Smith et al., 1992). In a policy context, however, the concept shows less mutability. Agrifood policies over the last sixty years are said to have been aimed at improving food security; at least, that is how they have been framed (Mooney and Hunt, 2009). What precisely these aims are and whether they reflect genuine food security will be addressed shortly. My point at the moment is simply that a relatively straightforward outline of the term can be discerned from the stated and implied aims of food and agricultural policy since the middle of the last century.

Let it also be clear that I use the term with a degree of hesitation. Like many scholars and practitioners (e.g. Lawrence and McMichael, 2012; Wittman et al., 2010), I am highly critical of the direction in which we have been led in its name, yet I am continually reminded during conversations with students and the general public that the term still has value. The term "food security", as detailed later, has been hijacked by a vocal and powerful minority. I use the word "hijacked" because in the process of being translated into policy it has turned into something with little resemblance to what I would call the original spirit of food security. As detailed in Chapter 2, the conceptual roots of food security extend back to President Roosevelt's now famous 1941 State of the Union address, where he spoke of "four essential freedoms" that tie all humans together: freedom of speech, of worship, from want, and from fear. Take, for example, my students, as the subject comes up repeatedly in my classes. For them, food security means more than just food *availability* and *access*. It equally speaks to issues of sustainability, enhanced individual, societal, and nutritional well-being, and prosperity. Yet that is not the food security enacted by many current agrifood policies and practices. What my students are referencing, rather, is food security's ancestral meaning—its spirit—borne out of Roosevelt's four freedoms speech. *That* understanding is worth reclaiming.

What does it mean to be food secure? Is that a reference to being secure *of* food or secure *through* food? Improvements have been made over the last half century toward making the world secure *of* food—though, admittedly, this doesn't bring much comfort for the roughly one billion people still classified as "hungry" (FAO, 2011). Globally, we seemingly have more calories than we know what to do with, as evidenced by the fact that we now "feed" *billions* annually to cars (as biofuels), cattle (as feed), and landfills (as waste). According to the Food and Agriculture Organization (FAO) of the United Nations (UN), the global food system produced 17 percent more calories per person at the dawn of the new millennium than it did thirty years earlier, even after factoring in a 70 percent population increase (FAO, 2002).

For decades, food security has been understood by the international community (and Western nations in particular) through the lens of the calorie. This productivist framing (Buttel, 2005) has effectively reduced the concept to a problem of production and insufficient technology utilization. The means and subsequently the ends under this framing are fairly straightforward and can be summed up in one word: *more*—more bushels per hectare, liters of milk per dairy cow, eggs per chicken, and the like. When assessed according to this frame, world agriculture has proven remarkably successful, as evidenced by the earlier statistic about the global food system's gains in per capita calorie production in the final quarter of the last century. Yet what are we to make of the precise *type* of calories being produced? In light of the so-called obesity epidemic (and rising rates of other diet-related health risks) as well as conventional agriculture's threat to environmental and public health, it is fair to ask whether these productivity "gains" have occurred at the expense of food security.

Another dominant food security frame centers on the rhetoric of free trade and trade liberalization (Mooney and Hunt, 2009). It is clear that even if we could produce all the calories needed to feed the Earth's human population—which, by the way, we already do!—without adequate *food access* hundreds of millions still risk going to bed hungry every night. This is in reference to a remark made by Henry Kissinger in his Keynote Address at the 1974 World Food Congress where he challenged the international community to ensure, within a decade, that "no child will go to bed hungry" (United Nations, 1975). Unfortunately, we have failed miserably at achieving this end, as hundreds of millions worldwide remain undernourished and a couple of hundred million more are malnourished (lacking the correct balance of macro- and micro-nutrients). Not that we should be surprised by any of this, as the steps we have taken over the last sixty years to enhance food security have been only tangentially related to food security's original spirit. The last thirty years, in particular, have produced unending waves of neoliberal "reforms" that have come crashing down on the world's small farmers, wiping most out in the process (Carolan, 2011b). These policies promised not only to make food widely available but to improve the purchasing power of consumers while ushering in a new era of growth, prosperity, and rising income for all. These promises have gone unfulfilled, as evidenced by the fact that hunger is the world's number-one health risk and that close to one billion still do not have enough to eat (FAO, nd).

People in abject hunger fit conventional understandings of what it means to be food insecure. They quite literally look the part. Must you, though, *look* and *feel* hungry to *be* food insecure? Take, for example, malnourished individuals—those whose diets are insufficient in certain essential micro-nutrients. They may not meet either of these characteristics. Malnourished individuals neither look the part—as malnourishment is a major risk factor for obesity—or feel it—as the *over*-consumption of highly processed foods is also correlated strongly with this state (Dumke, 2005). In the end, if a diet is clearly linked to ill health, what does it matter if under- or over-consumption is to blame? The final result in either case is the same: a shortened life and reduced well-being. Our understanding of food security ought to be updated to reflect these realities. Societies awash in cheap, highly processed, and nutritiously shallow calories ought to be rightfully categorized: as food insecure.

Food security, as currently conceived, operationalized, and measured in policy circles, leaves too much unquestioned. The FAO and World Health Organization (WHO) compile food security indicator statistics on things like the prevalence of underweight children under the age of five and the proportion of population below minimal levels of dietary energy consumption. Yet these data tell us absolutely nothing about the state of food security in high-income nations and at a minimum merely reinforce something we have long known: that incredibly impoverished countries are terribly food insecure. A UN-sponsored book titled *Food Security* recently remarked that "the extent of hunger and food insecurity [in the US] is much less severe than in the developing world" (Dutta and Gundersen, 2007, p. 44). In the space of less than one sentence the affluent US is extoled while the *entire* "developing" world is condemned on the basis of their respective levels of food security. Perhaps such pronouncements are empirically justified when food security is narrowly defined as, say, calories produced per capita. But would the statement still hold if food security started to be viewed through a "*through* food" lens, where human well-being became the end measured and not yields or calories per capita? I doubt it.

What, then, does it mean to think about food security through a "through food" lens? To answer this question let me ask this: what is the ultimate goal of food security—*food* or *security*? Is the endgame about promoting caloric or well-being abundance; is it about full-stomachs or full (and long) lives? For each of these questions I choose the latter option. And by the end of this book my guess is that you will, too (if you do not already).

Prior to writing this book I gave a number of public lectures about why we need to expand our conventional understanding of food security. During these events I occasionally encountered people who were uncomfortable with such an aim. Recently, for example, I had an exchange with an individual who took issue with my contention that understandings of food security cannot be divorced from well-being. Their question specifically was "What does food security have to do with measures of life-satisfaction?" I wanted to say, "Everything!", as it seems obvious to me that food security ought to be about making people better off. Instead I made a more tempered argument, noting how, on the one hand, someone cannot be happy with life when they are starving. On the other hand, we also know that the adage about never having too much of a good thing is patently false. Returns on welfare are diminishing for even something as essential as food. Once you become sufficiently well nourished any additional food, up to a point, might still improve your well-being but not to the same degree as it would have when you were underfed. Let us also remember that there is a point at which these returns stop, after which the relationship between societal and individual welfare and food consumption turns *negative*. These negative returns are experienced not only in an objective health sense (poor health) but also subjectively, as a growing body of research points to how affluence and abundance can actually cause stress, regret, status consumption behavior, and, when it comes to food, obesity and other diet-related health risks (Jackson, 2009; Kasser, 2002; Medez and Popkin, 2004; Schor, 2005).

I also have a problem with how conventional food security discourse treats less affluent countries, as if there is nothing we can learn from them. There is a tendency in the food security literature to hold up as exemplars—thanks to the aforementioned "secure *of* food" lens—countries that may not be deserving of either praise or emulation. Again, take the US. More than a third of its adults are defined as obese (CDC, nd). Avoidable annual food waste within this country amounts to over 55 million metric tonnes (that is nearly 29 percent of annual production!), which if consumed could save from being emitted at least 113 million metric tonnes of carbon-dioxide equivalents annually (Venkat, 2011). The annual total cost of pesticides alone in this nation, upon public health, the environment, and human communities, has been placed in the billions of dollars (Pimentel, 2005). And, as far as subjective well-being goes, the average citizen in the US reports far lower levels of life satisfaction than her counterpart in countries with significantly lower income levels and much higher food costs (Carolan, 2011b; Jackson, 2009). We could not emulate this model globally if we tried, as it is entirely unsustainable. But let us say, hypothetically, that we could. Given the points just mentioned, why would we *want* to?

The journey ahead

The book is organized around three sections. The first, consisting solely of Chapter 2, looks at the translation of food security from concept to policy directives and actual practices over roughly the last century. This move altered our understanding of the concept, taking it from something that was a means to an end (secure *through* food)—borne out of Roosevelt's four freedoms speech—to now an end in itself (secure *of* food) (see Figure 1.1). A distinct outline of food security can be discerned by looking at the stated and implied aims of agrifood policies during this timeframe, as they are often said to be in pursuit of its enhancement. As detailed in Chapter 2, this outline reflects three overlapping and cumulative foci:

1 the *calorie-ization of food security* (1940s to the present), where emphasis is placed on increasing agricultural output (e.g., the green revolution);
2 the *neoliberalization of food security* (1970s to the present), where the push is made for trade liberalization and global market integration; and
3 the *empty calorie-ization of food security* (1980s to the present), where for a variety of reasons—such as foreign direct investment (FDI) and the liberalization of marketing—processed foods take national food systems by storm.

These framings of food security are challenged in the book's second section. Against the food security yardstick created by these framings one could draw the conclusion that agrifood policy has been a resounding success—after all, the world has never seen such abundance of cheap calories. Yet these "gains" have come at tremendous cost to the environment, individual and societal well-being, human health, and the food sovereignty of nations (see, e.g., Carolan, 2011b; Sage, 2011). Chapter 3 looks at individual and societal well-being and nutrition, specifically examining how well the above-mentioned foci have enhanced (or more accurately detracted from) these ends. The national-level indicators of nutritional and human well-being utilized in this chapter include average life-expectancy and life-satisfaction statistics, the Human Development Index and the Happy

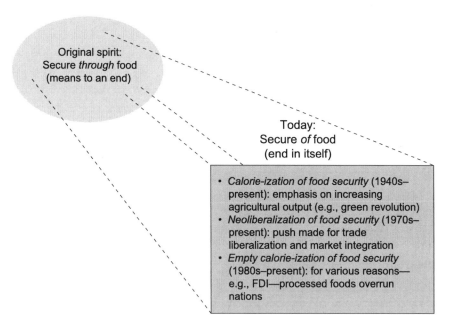

Figure 1.1 Changing understandings of food security.

Planet Index, and dietary data (specifically, daily per capita consumption of oils, fats, and sugars) from the WHO. Chapter 4 turns to the subject of sustainability, exploring specifically the toll presently being placed on the environment under the guise of food security. Many scholars and practitioners are careful not to divorce agroecology from their understandings of what it means to be food secure (Perfecto et al., 2009). Yet the fact that countries with clearly oversized ecological food-prints (the ecological footprint of an entire food system) are simultaneously lauded for their levels of food security is as unfortunate as it is telling. From a long-term food security perspective, large ecological footprints are fundamentally unsustainable and therefore ought to be avoided. Metrics examined in this chapter include issues related to energy use and greenhouse gas emissions, water use, food waste, and the production and consumption of meat and biofuels. Finally, in Part II, Chapter 5 looks at the phenomena of food sovereignty, safety, and access while making the case for their inclusion in future conceptualizations of food security. How dependent are countries upon others for their food? How concentrated are their agrifood chains? What about food and worker safety; what impacts have agrifood policies had upon these ends? And how reliant are producers upon agribusinesses for their agricultural inputs? These questions are explored in Chapter 5.

The third and final section—comprising Chapters 6 and 7—summarizes while gleaning lessons from the previous chapters. It is in this spirit that the Food and Human Security Index (FHSI) is introduced and discussed in Chapter 6. The FHSI takes into consideration indicators for the following states/conditions:

- individual and societal well-being;
- ecological sustainability;
- potential for food independence;
- nutritional well-being; and
- freedom in agrifood chain.

FHSI scores are calculated for 126 countries. To be clear, the FHSI is *not* a measure of food security. To measure food security would first require that I define it in precise terms. The spirit of food security, however, cannot be confined to any exact definitional box, though many have tried (Smith et al., 1992). As the word "spirit" implies, genuine food security is far too nebulous for definitional specificity; a quality we ought to value as it gives the concept flexibility, allowing it to take root in different social and ecological environments. One of the strengths of the FHSI is that it embraces many of the very concerns that at present cause so many to be critical of food security as currently performed. As an aggregate of some of the empirics introduced in the book's second section, the FHSI also offers an "objective" way to talk about those new lines of thought around food security that this book is looking to develop. The ranking of countries that emerges is surprising and counterintuitive, at least as far as conventional understandings of food security are concerned. Chapter 7 builds on this discussion while filling in important gaps. While starting at the level of the farm, this chapter focuses most of its attention beyond the farm gate, recognizing that food security is more than just about issues surrounding production. For example, this chapter addresses the important question "What can we eat if not GDP?" The chapter concludes by arguing for a thoroughly sociological rendering of food security. This position views food security not as a thing—or an end in itself—but as a process that ought to make people and the planet better off.

Part I

A failed project

Chapter 2

Food security

A brief history

Definitions of food security are like noses: everybody has one. One review from over twenty years ago yielded close to two hundred definitions (Smith et al., 1992), which means the literature today is populated with considerably more (recall from the previous chapter that a Google search generated roughly 19.7 million "hits"). Yet this chapter is not concerned with how food security is conceived by agrifood scholars. The focus of this chapter, rather, lies in more concrete matters: namely, in how food security has actually been *enacted* through agrifood policy. This exercise, admittedly, will require some interpretation as what has been said and what has been done in the name of food security are not always the same. An examination of the stated and implied aims of, and the consequences arising from, agrifood policies and practices over the last sixty years—as they have often been described as food security enhancing (Mooney and Hunt, 2009)—reveals an outline of the concept that is surprisingly stable.

Tracing this outline reveals three phases to how food security has been conceived in international policy circles over the years: the calorie-ization of food security (1940s to the present); the neoliberalization of food security (1970s to the present); and the empty calorie-ization of food security (1980s to the present). These phases should be understood as having developed through a process of cumulative continuity as opposed to disruption and change. The calorie-ization of food security, for example, has not been replaced but rather supplemented with additional directives and aims. Agrifood policy continues its obsession with the calorie. Yet, unlike fifty years ago, this obsession now has company.

With the help of this outline we can begin to understand why some look upon the present agrifood landscape with pride and others disgust. According to the food security yardstick sketched in this chapter, the last sixty years have been a resounding success—after all, world agriculture produces more calories per person than it did thirty years ago (17 percent more!). Yet do more calories, economic growth, and integrated global markets alone make for a secure food system? Lest we forget, the "gains" pointed to by proponents of the agrifood status quo come at tremendous cost to the environment, individual and societal well-being, human health, and the food sovereignty of nations (see, e.g., Carolan, 2011b; Dixon and Broom, 2007; Sage, 2011).

Calorie-ization of food security

For millennia, food scarcity plagued those lowest in the class hierarchy, a fact that was often met with indifference among those of higher social status. This began to change, however, with urbanization, industrialization, and nation building (Camporesi, 1989). In nineteenth-century Great Britain, the ruling class was confronted with the problem of how to feed the growing mass of workers streaming into cities from the countryside. They were not overcome with some newfound compassion toward those of lower social rank. Their interests, rather, centered more on self-preservation due to anxieties about social unrest. Such anxieties were articulated decades later in John Steinbeck's *The Grapes of Wrath*, when Tom Joad asks, "How can you frighten a man whose hunger is not only in his own cramped stomach but in the wretched bellies of his children? You can't scare him—he has known a fear beyond every other" (Steinbeck, 2006 [1939], p. 318). The goal, therefore, was not to feed the poor well but to feed them well *enough* to keep them from rioting in the streets. In the aptly titled book *Late Victorian Holocausts*, Mike Davis (2001) details the price paid by colony populations (like their outright starvation) as Great Britain sought cheap caloric fuel to feed the bodies of its underpaid working class. And for a time the most popular calories sought for this end were those derived from sugar.

Sydney Mintz (1985) delves into the historical relevance of sugar as a central element of early industrial expansion. The rate at which sugar entered the diets of the working poor in England in the nineteenth century is remarkable. Per capita consumption increased almost threefold, from approximately 30 pounds (14 kg) in 1800 to 90 pounds (41 kg) in 1900. By 1850, sugar consumption among the working class exceeded that of the upper class—a statistic made possible by a 50 percent reduction in the price of sugar between 1840 and 1870.

Why sugar? It is impossible to reduce its growing popularity in the rapidly industrializing countries of Europe and North America to any one variable. Sugar is in possession of certain characteristics, however, which undoubtedly helped its case. One of the more notable is the efficiency by which the sugarcane yields calories. A century ago, as Mintz points out, an acre of fertile tropical land planted in sugarcane yielded in excess of 8 million calories (compared to, for example, an acre of corn, which in 1921 yielded just over 3.2 million calories; Ohio State Horticultural Society, 1921). Once large sugar plantations were established on suitable lands throughout the British Empire, "the appeal of sucrose as a solution to food problems becomes almost irresistible" (Mintz, 1985, p. 191).

As for the calorie—it had only recently been born. Its first mention in the context of nutrition occurred in the late 1870s, though knowledge that food provided the human body with energy dates back further (the "heat unit" preceded the calorie, though the two are said to have shared the same value) (Ziegler, 1922). The calorie (and the heat unit before it) did to the agricultural sciences and nutrition what Newton's law of gravity did to physics: it legitimized the fields by reducing food to quantitative—a.k.a. "scientific"—terms. This in turn gave agrifood policy the veneer of objectivity, for by making the ultimate subject of concern calories—which made all agricultural commodities commensurable—policy-makers and politicians no longer needed to let things like culture, tastes, and local socio-ecological conditions influence the decision-making process.

The value of macro-nutrients—protein, fat, and carbohydrates—began to be extoled by the late nineteenth century, followed shortly thereafter with acknowledgement of "the vitamin principle" in the first years of the twentieth century (Grazer, 2005). However, while remarkably precise calculations could be made about the caloric value of food and the daily energy requirements of individuals, such specificity did not yet exist in discussions about macro- and micro-nutrients (a fact that has since changed considerably; see Box 2.1). The Illinois Farmers' Institute's *1911 Year Book*, for example, explains in exact terms the average amount of calories per hour consumed for such states as "man at rest, sleeping" (65), "man at moderately active muscular exercise" (290), and "man at very severe muscular exercise" (600) (McKeene, 1911, p. 168). Later, while explaining how "it is very simple to use such a table in calculating the number of calories which are spent in twenty-four hours under different body condition," the *Year Book* illustrates how one can calculate their daily caloric requirements (p. 168). In the example given, a "clerk or school teacher" that "sleeps for 9 hours," "works at desk 9 hours," "reads, writes, or studies 4 hours," and "walks or does light exercise 2 hours" burns approximately 2,225 calories a day. Later, the reader is told the daily calorie requirements of, for example, a shoemaker (2,000–2,400), weaver (2,400–2,700), farm laborer (in the busy season) (3,200–4,200), excavator (4,100–5,000), and lumberjack (over 5,000) (p. 169). This is soon followed with an extensive list of foods and sample meals, with each broken down to a precise caloric expression.

Box 2.1 The ideology of nutritionism

Nutritionism refers to a "quantitative logic" that "obscures the broader cultural, geographical, and ecological contexts in which foods, diets, and bodily health are situated" (Scrinis, 2008, p. 44). Rather than seeing food as part of a larger socio-material whole, nutritionism sees in food many smaller unconnected (and thus readily substitutable) material components. Nutritionism is in many respects an extension of the logic that originally gave rise to our fetishization of the calorie over a century ago.

Nutritionism is reflected in such "solutions" to malnutrition as Golden Rice—rice genetically engineered to possess high levels of vitamin A. Vitamin A, however, is fat soluble, so simply adding more of it to a diet already lacking dietary fat does not solve much. Moreover, Golden Rice ignores deeper "why" questions, such as: why is vitamin A deficiency increasing throughout parts of the world in the first place? Evaluating foods entirely by their material components also does violence to their deeper cultural connections. For example, breeding or genetically engineering a plant to enhance certain nutritional properties can alter its cooking and storage properties in addition to its taste, odor, color, and texture (John and Eyzaguirre, 2007).

Nutritionism is also reflected in the marketing strategies of the food industry, to its benefit. Food historian Marion Nestle (2007) tells of when General Mills began to fortify its boxed cereal during the late 1970s. While the practice cost the company an additional 7 cents per box, consumers were charged 36 cents more (a hefty mark-up back when you could buy a box for a little more than one US dollar).

More worrisome still is how this obsession over the material components of food distracts us from talking about the foods themselves and their relationship to such issues as social, public, and environmental health. I am reminded of a recent debate raging in the US court system between the high-fructose corn syrup and cane-sugar industries. The former are stating their product is chemically identical to sugar and they have rolled out an expensive advertising campaign claiming as much (as if being identical to sugar is now a health claim!). Thanks to nutritionism we are caught up debating whether corn syrup is identical to sugar rather than realizing what I would otherwise think is obvious: namely, that we need to consume *less of both*—and that whether they are identical is ultimately immaterial from a public and environmental health standpoint.

The calorie did not just dominate talk about food at this time; it came, as I've already indicated, to be largely *synonymous* with it. In a 1911 article in *Popular Science* the esteemed early twentieth-century animal scientist Dr. Henry Armsby (1911, p. 469) writes: "Now the problem of food supply is in essence a problem of energy supply. Food yields the energy which operates the bodily mechanism and upon the regularity and sufficiency of this energy supply depends absolutely all human endeavor. To produce those carriers of energy which we call foods is the chief function of the farmer." Or take the rather striking chart reproduced in Table 2.1, coming from the 1921 *Proceedings of the Annual Meeting of the Ohio State Horticultural Society* (Ohio State Horticultural Society, 1921, p. 41). Note specifically its title: "'Food value' per acre." While protein is highlighted alongside calories, the text accompanying the chart makes it clear which of the two is most important when speaking of food's ultimate value: the calorie. Corn, for example, is described as "one of our best food producing crops" (p. 40) due to the copious calories it yields, followed by calorically dense cherries, which "are next in food producing value to corn" (p. 41).

As Table 2.1 makes clear, macro-nutrients were already valued in the early decades of the twentieth century, so it would be a bit of an

Table 2.1 "Food value" per acre, 1921

	Lbs. per acre	Total protein	Total calories
Corn	2,128	159.6	3,287,760
Cherries	9,000	81.0	3,105,000
Cabbage	24,000	336	3,000,000
Turnips	16,000	208	2,960,000
Peaches	12,000	84.0	2,640,000
Apples	10,800	32.4	2,376,000
Oranges	13,345	80.07	2,268,650
Wheat	1,620	140.76	1,708,500
Grapes	5,000	50	1,675,000
Tomatoes	14,000	126	1,470,000
Strawberries	3,200	28.8	560,000

Source: Adapted from Ohio State Horticultural Society, 1921

overstatement to claim that only calories mattered. A League of Nations document from 1937, for example, criticizes one unnamed country that has "difficulty in distinguishing between promotion of good dietary habits and stimulation of demand for home-grown agricultural products" (Eliot and Heseltine, 1937, p. 332). The report continues: "For example, in a country where the production of, and trade in, sugar are a state monopoly, a governmental department distributed a sixteen-page pamphlet 'giving a brief description of the important part played by sugar in public health as an article of mass consumption'" (p. 332). Yet, as sugar was on its way out, a new category of calories came to prominence: namely, those derived from cereals (wheat, rice, and the like). These calories became somewhat of a *cause célèbre* with the green revolution, which directed world agriculture toward their large-scale production. This can be seen plainly enough in the Food and Agriculture Organization's (FAO) definition of food security in 1974, where it is said to involve "ensuring, to the utmost, the availability at all times of adequate world supplies of basic food stuffs, *primarily cereals*, so as to avoid acute food shortages in the event of widespread crop failures or national disasters, sustain a steady expansion of production and consumption, and reduce fluctuation in production and prices" (quoted in Shaw, 2007, p. 150; my emphasis).

The avoidance of raw, unadulterated hunger—of making sure people have something (indeed anything) to eat—has been a long-standing goal within the international community. In the early 1930s the Health Division of the League of Nations was charged with assessing the food situation among represented countries. The resulting publication, *Nutrition and Public Health* (1935), represents arguably the first account of hunger in an international context (Shaw, 2007). With member nations locked in the grip of the Great Depression, the report offered a stark reminder that the so-called modern age, in terms of sheer numbers, was filled with as many hungry bodies (perhaps more) as any that had preceded it.

A few years later, in 1941, President Roosevelt gave perhaps the most famous State of the Union address of the twentieth century. In this speech, Roosevelt identifies "four essential freedoms" that are shared "everywhere in the world": freedom of speech; of worship; from want; and from fear. The founding conference of the FAO of the United Nations in 1943 took Roosevelt's call to heart as it looked specifically "to consider the goal of freedom from want in relation to food and agriculture" (FAO, 1943, p. 1). One could locate the original spirit of food security within these four essential freedoms. In doing this, it is understood to be but a means to an even more profound end—namely, the enhancement of individual and societal freedom and well-being. This original spirit, however, was soon forgotten as means began to be mistaken for ends.

While not using the term "food security" outright, the organizers get close, as the proceedings discuss the need to "secure [a] suitable supply of food" (p. 1). Characterized as freedom from want, we find here one of the earliest conceptual framings of food security: essentially, the absence of abject hunger. For a variety of reasons, this "want" was viewed principally as the result of under-productivity, most notably in less affluent parts of the world (though farmers in affluent nations were also encouraged to intensify their operations or risk falling off the agricultural treadmill; Cochrane, 1993). The solution, then, was simple: agricultural systems needed to produce more (referred to elsewhere as the "productivist ideology"; see, e.g., Buttel, 2005). The green revolution represents the actualization of a policy and research agenda informed heavily by this calorie-ization of food security. It was enacted through a series of research and technology transfer initiatives, with support from the Rockefeller and Ford foundations, which took place immediately following World War II and lasted into the 1970s. The primary goal of these initiatives centered on the development of high-yield varieties of a handful of cereals, which also required the expansion of the necessary irrigation infrastructures and input supply chains (fertilizer, pesticides, seeds, etc.).

This resulted in new varieties of rice, wheat, and corn that proved highly responsive to synthetic fertilizers and irrigation. The new varieties were quickly adopted in many parts of the developing world, leading to dramatic increases in food production.

In terms of caloric output the green revolution was massively successful. Total food production in developing countries more than doubled between 1960 and 1985, meaning it grew at rates faster than population growth. However, after factoring in all the calories used as inputs—such as petroleum, the energy used to manufacture and transport fertilizer and pesticides, and the electricity used to operate pumps for irrigation—"modern" agricultural systems fair considerably less well in terms of their overall net output. For example, for each calorie of energy in 1945 used to grow corn, 3.7 calories of corn were produced, whereas by 1970 that ratio had dropped to 1 to 2.8 (Pimentel et al., 1973).

While the green revolution can be credited with helping bring forth remarkable productivity gains (at least in some parts of the world), it can be equally lambasted for its failure to make necessary social, political, and economic gains. This failure took two forms. The first involved its explicit emphasis on technological solutions, believing, essentially, that we could (plant) breed our way to food security. The other, related to the first, was that the green revolution's implicit technological optimism led to apathy in many circles for a need to create broader *social* change. For example, in 1985 the head of the international body overseeing green revolution research, Syed Shahid Husain, argued that gains in productivity were all the poor required and that "added emphasis on poverty alleviation is not necessary" (quoted in Lappe and Collins, 1986, p. 49).

The green revolution may also have forestalled many of the very reforms that we know (with hindsight) promote prosperity and food security, especially among the rural poor. Critics of the green revolution have argued that it reduced pressure for radical political change in Asia and Latin America by promoting technological innovation, market integration, and scale increases (Gonzalez, 2004). Its rise coincided with the growth of peasant movements in the Philippines, Indonesia, Malaysia, Vietnam, and India, and land reform movements in Latin America. But the green revolution likely put a halt to many of these movements and the broader social transformations they looked to spawn. As one study on the subject from the early 1970s notes, "There has been no substantial recent land reform at all in the other major countries affected by the green revolution"

(Cleaver, 1972, p. 178). This was due to the fact that the green revolution further empowered the landed elite while simultaneously marginalizing the smallholder and landless peasant (de Janvry and Sadoulet, 1989). Countries where land was more equitably distributed in 1980 made greater advances in reducing food insecurity over the last two decades of the century than countries where land ownership was more concentrated (Gonzalez, 2004). As for countries where the green revolution took deepest root during this period, land inequities *increased* (Lappe and Collins, 1986). An article in the *American Journal of Agricultural Economics* finds "a significant negative relationship" between an unequal distribution of agricultural land and output per hectare, an effect that persists even after controlling for input use, land quality, human capital, and agricultural research effort (Vollrath, 2007, p. 202). And it is not just levels of food security that are hampered by land inequality. A working paper by the International Monetary Fund (IMF) concludes that "land inequality has been shown to have a negative impact on other key aspects of economic development—education, institutions and financial development—and on poverty" (Vollrath and Erickson, 2007).

The green revolution, like any policy or program, had winners and losers. It made matters worse for the most vulnerable classes by disproportionately benefiting large farmers without countervailing social and economic reforms directed specifically at improving the welfare of the rural poor. It required significant capital investment. Even when seeds were provided for free or at a subsidized rate maximum yields were predicated on the application of key inputs— namely, fertilizers and irrigation—at precise application rates and times. Access to these inputs, however, requires capital and credit. In turn, these inputs promote indiscriminate plant growth: namely, weeds. Chemical herbicides thus became yet another necessary input to be purchased by the farmer. The green revolution is also responsible for replacing the dazzling panoply of biodiversity once found in agroecosystems around the world with a handful of high-yielding varieties. Ten crops now account for 70 to 80 percent of all calories consumed globally (Clay, 2011), a genetic uniformity that renders modern agroecosystems vulnerable to insects and disease. So we can add insecticides and fungicides to the list of capital inputs that must now be purchased thanks to the green revolution. Further complicating matters are recent changes promoted under the guise of neoliberalism (to be discussed shortly), which have resulted in the elimination of government institutions and programs directed at providing agricultural credit, technical assistance, and marketing support for the rural poor in less affluent nations.

This interest directed at increasing yields was not duplicated, however, when the subject turned to job creation. One could even argue that the green revolution was more interested in *eliminating* rural jobs than creating them, as many of the aforementioned capital investments intentionally reduced the need for rural labor (e.g., herbicides replaced manual weeding) so farm scale could grow. The green revolution was dangerously myopic in its focus, as lower food prices do not enhance welfare if they accompany joblessness. Roughly 80 percent of the world's poor (and hungry) reside in rural areas in less affluent countries. The livelihoods of smallholders and tenant farmers often hinge on the ability to sell their agricultural output. Lower agricultural commodity prices that followed the green revolution therefore result in lower incomes for many of the world's rural poor—a problem that could have been substantially alleviated had countervailing policies and programs been implemented. The green revolution was also hard on that segment of the rural poor who do not own land: the landless laborers—the poorest of the rural poor—as it left them both landless *and* laborless. A review from 1995 examining over three hundred studies published from 1970 to 1989 on the social and economic effects of the green revolution finds 80 percent to have concluded that it has been *detrimental* to rural poverty and inequality (Freebairn, 1995).

Moreover, the aforementioned productivity gains require some qualification. The yield increases in Asia linked to the green revolution were largely the result of the region's considerable rainfall and extensive river system, which supports large-scale irrigation systems. Contrast this to dry sub-Saharan Africa. Eighty-five percent of Kenya's arable land, for example, cannot be irrigated as it is too far from any significant water source and thus must rely upon intermittent rainfall. Then there is the problem of dietary diversity (or increasingly the lack thereof), as illustrated in the earlier statistic about fewer than a dozen crops now feeding the majority of the world's population (Clay, 2011). Crops bred for higher yields have displaced traditional crops that are—or were, as some are now extinct—higher in iron and other micro-nutrients. In South Asia, for example, cereal production has increased more than fourfold since 1970, while production of pulses (high-protein legumes) has dropped 20 percent (Gupta and Seth, 2007; Welsh and Graham, 1999). Furthermore, how cereals are processed prior to consumption has further deleterious effects on diet.

Rice, in particular, is consumed after milling, which removes precious micro-nutrients. Compare this to pulses, one-time food staples that are disappearing from diets around the world. Pulses are traditionally consumed whole after cooking, a practice that keeps their micro-nutrient profile intact (Cordain, 1999).

Recall the FAO's foundational principle—of creating a freedom from want as it applies to food—which is directed at the achievement of deeper goals masterfully laid out by Roosevelt in his 1941 State of the Union address. What this principle seeks to achieve, to put it in language used in the previous chapter, is security *through* food. The green revolution is a technological response to this goal, which in the end has caused us to mistake means for ends. The logic of the green revolution is that if we produce more and make "secure *of* food" the goal, the aim of being "secure *through* food" will naturally take care of itself. And by "more" I am talking specifically about calories derived from cereals. The reality of the calorie-ization of food security is scattered throughout the literature. In a peer-reviewed article co-authored by a United States Department of Agriculture (USDA) plant scientist, the green revolution is described as making a "push toward food (i.e. calorie or energy) security" (Welsh and Graham, 1999, p. 9; my emphasis). More recently, the USDA's (2011, p. 2; my emphasis) *International Food Security Assessment 2011–21* explains in its methods section that the "[c]ommodities covered in this report include grains [which make up the vast majority of calories assessed], root crops, and 'other' . . . These three groups account for 100 percent of all calories consumed in the study countries and are expressed in grain equivalent. The conversion is based on *calorie content.*"

Additional deleterious effects of mistaking calorie security for food security can be found by looking at changes in the livestock industry—or, more accurately, changes to livestock themselves. Livestock today, for a variety of reasons, grow larger and faster than their ancestors. Chickens, for instance, now require twenty-seven fewer days—and almost 50 percent less feed—to reach slaughter weight than was needed in 1950 (Catel, 2011). Yet how do today's highly efficient industrial chickens compare to their ancestors in terms of the quantity and type of calories yielded? Figure 2.1 plots the total kcal per 100 grams of chicken from 1870 to 2004 (Wang et al., 2009). As the figure illustrates, chickens are becoming more calorically dense, an expected trend given agrifood policies' aforementioned emphasis on caloric output. Yet how can 100 grams of chicken contain almost

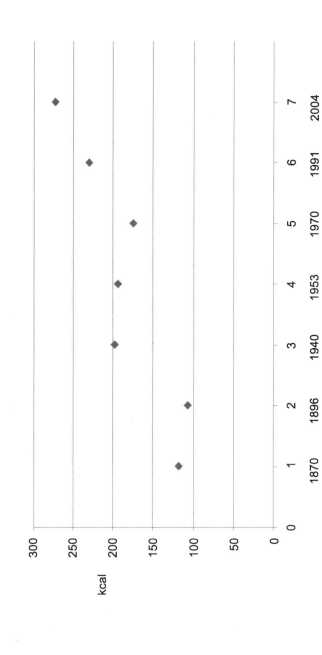

Figure 2.1 Total kcal per 100 grams of chicken for select years.

Source: Adapted from Wang et al., 2009.

150 percent more calories today than it did in 1870? The answer is in the fat.

Today's conventional chicken is considerably fatter than its ancestors. Let us look first at how the animal's protein content has changed. Kcal of protein per 100 grams of chicken from 1870 to 2004 is detailed in Figure 2.2. Note the downward trend. The opposite can be said for the fat content of these birds. Not only do today's chickens carry less protein per 100 grams but, as shown in Figure 2.3, they also carry remarkably more fat than in decades past. Moreover, while not shown in the latter figure, it is worth noting that the *type* of fat has also changed. Chickens today are not only fatter but possess a higher percentage of "bad" and a lower percentage of "good" fats than the chickens eaten by our ancestors.

Neoliberalization of food security

The story of food security does not end with the green revolution. Even diehard proponents of productivism realized that astronomical increases in agricultural output could never feed the world if those calories were not efficiently allocated. And as the market has long been viewed as *the* mechanism for the efficient allocation of resources, a concerted push simultaneously took place in the mid to late twentieth century (most notably from the 1970s to the present) to increase the integration of international markets for agricultural commodities—a theme I refer to as the neoliberalization of food security.

But first: neoliberalism—what is it? As opposed to classic liberalism, where individual liberties are privileged above all else—even if that means involving the state to enhance and protect them—neoliberalism sanctifies free enterprise while minimizing as much as possible the role of the state. Though its emergence and evolution are complicated (Harvey, 2005), certain geopolitical factors in the 1930s and 1940s (e.g., the rise of fascism in Italy and Germany and the brutal regime led by Stalin in Russia) helped convince a handful of influential world leaders that classic liberalism needed to be replaced with a new type of liberalism—hence the moniker *neo*liberalism (Busch, 2010). Neoliberalism claims to reject all types of central planning, leaving everything to be decided by the market; though, as others have pointed out (Busch, 2010), this new liberalism actually requires *more* central planning as its apparatuses run on legal and regulatory tracks erected by the state.

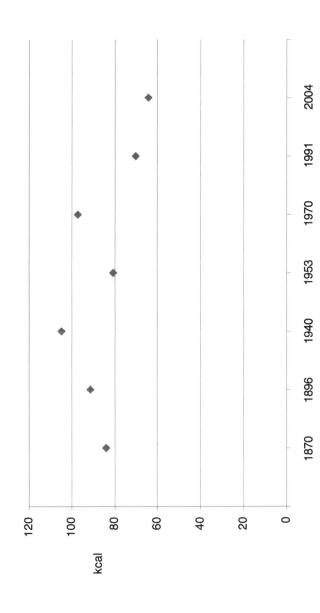

Figure 2.2 Kcal of protein per 100 grams of chicken for select years.

Source: Adapted from Wang et al., 2009.

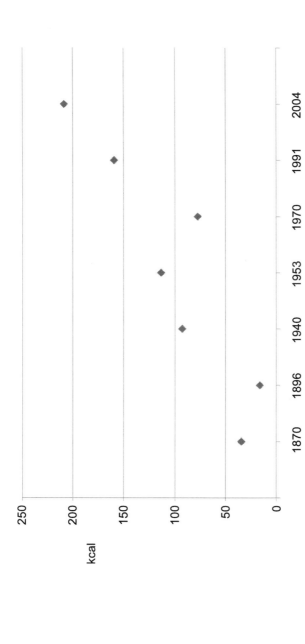

Figure 2.3 Kcal of fat per 100 grams of chicken for select years.

Source: Adapted from Wang et al., 2009.

With the neoliberalization of food security, countries were not all expected, nor were they even encouraged, to become self-sufficient in food production terms. Many were in fact aggressively instructed—with a variety of carrots and sticks—to abandon policies directed at such ends. For example, in 2002, the then deputy director-general of the World Trade Organization (WTO), Miguel Rodríguez Mendoza, argued that national food security strategies could be achieved only through international trade:

> History has shown that food security does not equal self-sufficiency of a country. It has more to do with international trade in food products that makes them available at competitive prices and sets the right incentives for those countries where they can be produced most efficiently. Food shortages have to do with poverty rather than with being a net food importer. Food security nowadays lies not only in the local production of food, but in a country's ability to finance imports of food through exports of other goods.
>
> (WTO, 2002)

As alluded to in this quote, food security, as conventionally understood, has little to do with farmer security, especially when talking about smallholders in low-income countries. Quite often policies claiming to be in pursuit of the former have been detrimental to the latter, which explains why hundreds of millions of small-scale peasant farmers have been pushed out of agriculture in recent decades (Bello, 2008; Carolan, 2011b). Former US Secretary of Agriculture John Block made just this point in 1986, proclaiming, "The idea that developing countries should feed themselves is an anachronism from a bygone era. They could better ensure their food security by relying on US agricultural products, which are available in most cases at lower cost" (quoted in Bello, 2008, p. 452).

Faith in the market to deliver cheap calories continually to the world's hungry is so great that countries have been instructed to abandon longstanding practices of surplus storage. Many governments have further been told (or one could even say "forced") by international organizations like the World Bank and the IMF to abandon policies that previously helped support a robust domestic agricultural sector. This has led to the dismantling of marketing boards, the elimination of subsidies for things like seed and fertilizer, and the canceling of government credit programs for small-scale farmers. Numerous countries that were at one time net exporters and/or food self-sufficient have recently experienced a significant decline in domestic production as their borders have been flooded with cheap imports from high-income nations that continue to subsidize their agricultural sectors heavily. Millions of small-scale farmers, subject to this unfair competition, have thus had little choice but to abandon agriculture. While done in the name of food security, the outcomes of these policies—whether in terms of farm incomes, human well-being, or national food sovereignty—suggest otherwise. The shortsightedness of these strategies has become particularly clear with the recent volatility in food prices. Given that low-income households spend close to (or in some cases more than) half of their disposable annual incomes on food, price increases of the magnitude witnessed in recent years have crippled many of the world's poor.

Between 1950 and 1970, low-income nations went from being entirely food self-sufficient to accounting for almost half of the world's grain imports (Friedmann, 1990, p. 20). Harriet Friedmann (1992) gives a thorough account of the growth of food dependency through an analysis of the global wheat trade, noting that before World War II no African, Latin American, or South Asian country imported the commodity. Now all countries within these regions rely to various degrees upon wheat imports. For example, whereas Nigeria was entirely food independent through the 1960s, by 1983 one-quarter of its total earnings went on importing wheat (Jarosz, 2009).

Many less affluent nations were well on their way in the middle of the last century to building a resilient food system, that is, until understandings of food security began to be overrun by the ideology of neoliberalism. Take the case of Zimbabwe. Programs in place from the 1940s to 1991 created unique public–private partnerships to provide high-quality, low-cost seed to small-scale farmers. In this arrangement, government breeders would experiment with hybrid seed, looking for varieties that performed well under adverse agroecological conditions. Lacking the capacity to produce and distribute high-performing varieties, the state would then rely upon private seed firms to mass-produce and distribute the improved seeds to farmers at prices set (and subsidized) by the government. However, the World Bank promised that a more competitive market for seed would increase supply and decrease production costs for farmers, so this arrangement was dismantled in the 1990s. This proved disastrous for small-scale Zimbabwean farmers. As the country's economy integrated itself into the global market the value of the Zimbabwean currency fell through the floor (currency devaluation is one of the many required bitter pills that developing economies must swallow in the name of neoliberalization in order to make their markets more attractive to foreign investment). As a result, the price of agricultural inputs increased from between 100 percent (in the case of seed and pesticides) to 700 percent (in the case of fertilizer) over the course of just one year (Zerbe, 2009). "The tragic irony of the privatization and liberalization of Zimbabwe's seed industry," in the words of one scholar, "is the fact that polices intended to promote agriculture production as a mechanism for addressing rural poverty actually wound up exacerbating rural poverty, undermining smallholder production, and reducing food security" (Zerbe, 2009, p. 168).

As for the liberalizing process itself, not all countries, it seems, have to play by the same rules. The 1947 General Agreement on Tariffs and Trade (GATT), which lasted until 1993, and was then replaced by the WTO in 1995, was weak on the subject of agricultural commodities. This gave countries considerable leeway as they set up policies and programs to protect and bolster national food systems. By the late 1980s and early 1990s, during the so-called Uruguay Round of multilateral trade negotiations of the GATT, agriculture came increasingly into the crosshairs of the negotiating parties, eventually giving birth (in 1995) to the Agreement on Agriculture (AoA). Though explicitly intended to correct market distortions in the agricultural sector, the AoA contains ambiguities and exceptions enabling countries like the US and economic regions such as the EU to maintain protectionist import barriers and trade-distorting subsidies. For example, while developing countries were required to eviscerate many of their government-funded initiatives, such as their agricultural credit programs and farm subsidies (both of which helped small-scale farmers tremendously), subsidy levels in industrialized countries *increased* after the AoA came into effect. There would seem to be a double standard ingrained—a "do as I say, not as I do" logic—in trade-oriented understandings of food security today.

Many proponents of trade liberalization also criticize the double standard that has emerged between the agricultural sectors of affluent nations (save, perhaps, for New Zealand, where agricultural subsidies have largely been eliminated) and the rest of the world. Where I differ from them is on the subject of where to go from here. Those who believe in the underlying logic of the neoliberalization of food security would argue that what we need is *more* liberalized trade. Yet the data (and history) do not support the thesis that more neoliberalization will bring enhanced food security. In fact, there is strong evidence that it would have the opposite effect.

First, more trade liberalization would do nothing to correct the distortions and inequities *already caused* by the concentration of agricultural markets thanks to policies up to this point. Due to this concentration, firms are able to exert considerable monopolistic and monopsonistic power (seller and buyer power, respectively) over other actors in the food system (buyer and seller power and market concentration in the agrifood chain are discussed in Chapter 5) (Carolan, 2011b). More neoliberalization is not going to reverse this concentration. If anything, it will exacerbate it.

Another limitation of liberalization is that it discourages the economic and biological diversification necessary to promote genuine food security at the national level. Contrary to the neoliberal prescriptions of institutions like the IMF, the World Bank, and the WTO, affluent nations achieved their economic dominance thanks, in part, to the use of subsidies and tariffs, the regulation of foreign investment, and other country-specific policy "flexibilities": the very macroeconomic tools that are now denied to low- and middle-income nations. The most food insecure countries are those that rely on one or two agricultural commodities to finance the importation of food products. Yet this is precisely what developing countries are being instructed to do—namely, to focus on the production of one or two commodities, the so-called law of comparative advantage.

Contrary to the specialization promoted by comparative advantage, genuine food security lies, at least in part, in *diversifying* production. If we have learned anything from the last decade, it is that countries cannot become overly reliant upon one or two agricultural export commodities for their foreign exchange earnings. This logic, however, should have been apparent over a hundred years ago. As early as the 1880s, countries that specialized in agricultural exports faced declining terms of trade for agricultural products relative to manufactured goods (Gonzalez, 2004). These countries found themselves on an economic treadmill of sorts, where they continually had to expand export production in order to keep up with the increasing price of manufactured imports. For example, between 1980 and 1998, the terms of trade between agricultural commodities and manufactured goods declined by more than 40 percent (Gonzalez, 2004). In addition, agricultural commodity prices have long varied considerably—especially relative to manufactured goods—robbing these countries of stable and predictable revenue streams, which made productive and social investments more risky.

The law of comparative advantage also actively discourages biological diversity. As countries are encouraged to specialize, biodiversity naturally suffers, leading to yet another type of dependency (see Box 2.2). The blanketing of landscapes with monocultures makes farmers within these economies dependent upon agribusinesses for their inputs as the productive ecological base of the nation erodes. There is good reason to be concerned that the wholesale elimination of subsidies around the world would result in further increases in crop specialization, as this is what the law of comparative advantage prescribes.

Box 2.2 Biocultural diversity loss

A term that has received increasing attention of late is "biocultural diversity." This is the full-throated acknowledgement that biodiversity sustains culture and vice versa. After all, it is through long-held cultural practices (agri*culture*) that much of the world's agrobiodiversity has been allowed to persist. The erosion, then, of those practices and the corresponding knowledges they help create has a direct impact on biodiversity levels. It is therefore no coincidence that most of the world's biodiversity hotspots are also cultural hotspots, represented by a concentration of divergent ethnic groups, linguistic diversity, and a rich array of cultural practices and folk knowledge.

Anthropologist Virginia Nazarea (1998) has studied sweet potato farmers in the Philippines extensively. One site she visited was in the process of converting to commercialized production, while at another they continued to produce at the level of subsistence. She had originally hypothesized that commercialization causes a narrowing of genetic and cultural diversity among the sweet potatoes grown. While this hypothesis was confirmed, Nazarea also discovered something unexpected. There was a large disparity between the two sites in terms of the number of varieties known or remembered, compared to the biodiversity that actually existed. The farmers at the commercial site had knowledge of a far lower percentage of sweet potato varieties than those at the other site. This suggests that cultural knowledge erodes even faster than genetic diversity itself. Reflecting upon her research, Nazarea (2005, p. 62) writes that this finding signified "that in the context of agricultural development and market integration, knowledge may actually be the first to go."

Knowledge, especially cultural knowledge, has to be used. While the green revolution certainly uses knowledge, it uses only certain types (Carolan, 2011a). Any knowledge not used is quickly forgotten, which means understandings about alternative methods of agriculture and the crops those traditional systems cultivated risk being lost with the spread of the green revolution. The importance of practice—of actually putting knowledge to work—is what DeLind (2006, p. 134) was getting at when she wrote, "knowledge that is not used, and information that is not felt, are indistinguishable from ignorance."

Finally, arguments for more liberalization ignore certain ecological realities that are present thanks largely to liberal policies already in place. Take, for example, the case involving the African country of Malawi. For years, the country suffered from persistent famine. In 2005, after one particularly disastrous corn harvest, 5 million of the county's 13 million residents needed emergency food aid. Yet, by 2007, Malawi was turning away food aid. So what was different? Fertilizer subsidies. The World Bank, the neoliberalism police of the global economy, had been leaning heavily on the Malawi government since the 1980s to eliminate its practice of providing fertilizer subsidies to the country's smallholders. This strategy, however, proved disastrous to poorer Malawian farmers, who were unable to afford fertilizer once the subsidy was eliminated. The country is plagued with gravely depleted soils, thanks in part to it having been "mined" to raise commodities for global export. Fertilizer is thus a necessity for the farmers, at least in the short term, until soil fertility is built up. Not surprisingly, then, the removal of the subsidy drastically slashed the productivity and thus incomes of those households already at risk of being food insecure. In defiance of the World Bank, Malawi's president, Bingu wa Mutharika, decided after the 2005 harvest to reintroduce the fertilizer subsidies, a move that notably improved the nutritional well-being of millions of the country's citizens.

Empty calorie-ization of food security

The neoliberalization of food security also helped to give rise to the liberalization of finance, which has increased the rate of foreign direct investment (FDI). FDI is investment by a firm in one country into a business located in another, leading to the former owning a substantial, but not necessarily a majority, interest (Hawkes, 2005). It is one of the primary mechanisms by which companies enter new markets. The rise of FDI marks yet another evolution in agrifood policy's response to hunger—what I call the empty calorie-ization of food security (see Box 2.3).

Box 2.3 Empty calories and the withering of the state

While this section focuses almost exclusively on FDI, it is important to remember that neoliberalism's effect on diet is complex and, when all the dots are connected, noticeably significant. As mentioned earlier, a stated aim of neoliberalism is to weaken the state—effectively to hollow it out—in the hope of making the market the sole arbiter of social life. This has had an incredibly perverse impact on what we eat. Take the example of public schools. In many countries—but especially the US—public educational systems are seeing their budgets slashed as a consequence of the state not living up to its fiduciary responsibilities due to forces attempting to restrict its reach. Administrators therefore now have to turn to private firms to fill coffers that previously were filled with public monies. This has resulted in things like "pouring rights," where schools receive large payments from soft-drink companies in exchange for the right to sell that company's—and *only* that company's—products. Not surprisingly, these rights are wrong from a public health standpoint as they result in the (over)consumption of empty calories (Nestle, 2000).

Or take the effect of neoliberalism on Farm to School programs, which seek to bring fresh, local produce to schools. On the face of it, this sounds like a win–win: farmers receive a higher premium price for their products by selling directly to schools; schools and school-aged children receive a seemingly safe, fresh, quality product. Unfortunately, as schools attempt to keep up with growing enrollments, the school kitchen is often

---

the last to expand as whatever scarce monies are available are directed to programs being evaluated by standardized tests (as monies tend to follow test scores). Many kitchens have thus had to switch to a "heat and serve" arrangement—that is, rows of microwaves—as they do not have the space to prepare food any more. FTS programs, however, presuppose space for preparation—after all, the food arrives fresh. To deal with this problem, some schools have asked FTS programs to provide *processed* foods (Allen and Guthman, 2006).

Between 1988 and 1997, food industry FDI increased from US$743 million to US$2.1 billion in Asia and from US$222 million to US$3.3 billion in Latin America—totals that far and away outstripped investments in agriculture in these regions. Food companies in the US generate revenue that is at least five times higher through FDI sales than through export sales (Rayner et al., 2007). Highly processed foods possess certain characteristics that make them ideal for FDI. For example, relative to trade, FDI can be a cost-effective way for firms to reach foreign food markets. Exporting highly processed foods can be cost prohibitive as transport and storage costs relative to the value of the product are high. Producing these foods in the host country for domestic distribution avoids many such costs. FDI also optimizes the effectiveness of branding and promotional marketing, allowing companies—such as Nestlé, Coca-Cola, and McDonald's—to benefit from economies of scale in marketing and advertising. Investing in well-known domestic brands is also advantageous for firms by giving them instant ownership over a brand already known in regional and/or national markets (Hawkes, 2005).

The rise of FDI has unquestionably led to the spread of nutritiously shallow calories. In Argentina, for example, 18 percent of all food expenditures were on meals eaten outside the home in 1996, up from a mere 8 percent in 1970. This increase correlates strongly with an increase in FDI in restaurant (and coffee, doughnut, ice-cream, etc.) chains and processed foods in the country (Hawkes, 2005). Or take Brazil, where growth in the sales of hamburgers, pre-made desserts, yoghurts, and flavored milk averaged 27 percent between 1993 and 1997, compared with 5 percent for such items as vegetable oils, margarines, poultry, and pork. In other words, dietary patterns—and thus consumer "choice"—track remarkably close with FDI trends (Farina, 2001; Zimmerman, 2011).

In the late 1990s and early 2000s nearly three-quarters of all FDI into Mexico was directed at the production of processed foods. During this period sales of "snacks" increased annually by roughly 12 percent, while "baked goods" saw a 55 percent increase (Hawkes, 2005). More remarkable still is the increase in carbonated soft-drink consumption in this country, which grew from 44 to 61 kcal per capita per day between 1992 and 2000 (Arroyo et al., 2004). As for the consumption of Coca-Cola drinks, this increased from 275 8-oz servings per person per year in 1992 to 487 8-oz servings in 2002 (that is more than the US per person average—436 servings—recorded at the time) (Hawkes, 2005).

There is a sizable body of research that looks specifically at how the North American Free Trade Agreement (NAFTA) has shaped Mexico's food-scape toward the production of empty calories and FDI. NAFTA, which came into force on January 1, 1994, liberalized not just "trade" but also investment rules. Mexico is now the third-largest recipient of US FDI in the processed food and beverage industries (Clark et al., 2012). Liberalized FDI has made the entry of large food retailers (and their highly processed wares) into Mexico easier. Prior to NAFTA, the average Mexican tariff on imports was 17.5 percent, which would have priced most foreign food products out of the market. These products—many of which were (and are) calorically empty—are now ubiquitous in Mexico, since the elimination of such trade barriers.

Food consumption patterns have changed dramatically in Mexico since 1994, shifting away from traditional food staples toward energy-dense, processed foods and animal-based products, all of which tend to be higher in fats, sugars, and calories. From 1988 to 1999 the average Mexican diet went from having 23.5 percent to 30.3 percent of its calories coming from fat (a 28.9 percent increase). During the same period, calories from carbohydrates declined from 59.7 percent to 57.5 percent of total calories consumed. Digging a little deeper in the data, however, shows consumption of *refined* carbohydrates increased, rising by 6.3 percent between 1984 and 1998 (no doubt thanks in part to rising levels of soda consumption) (Rivera et al., 2004). These trends help us understand why Mexico ranks second behind the US in a 2010 OECD (Organization for Economic Cooperation and Development) report ranking forty countries according to the proportion of their populations who are obese (cited in Clark et al., 2012).

The question remains, however: are these changes simply a function of rising prosperity or the result of trade policy? A recent article in the *International Journal of Occupational and Environmental Health* argues that a significant amount of blame can indeed be laid at the feet of NAFTA. Among other things, the authors point out that "the increased consumption of obesogenic [obesity-promoting] foods in Mexico, much as in the United States, is a trend among all socio-economic groups (both urban and rural), not only the wealthy living in cities" (Clark et al., 2012, p. 62).

FDI has also been linked to the tremendous global growth in the consumption of French fries and frozen potato products more generally (Plummer and Makki, 2002). FDI patterns are radically restructuring potato farming around the world. McDonald's, for example, has invested heavily in potato processing plants in Argentina to supply French fries to its restaurants in the country. This has subsequently affected supply chains, as affiliated processors now contract with local potato farmers, a practice that inherently favors larger operators over small-scale farmers (Farina, 2001).

While the general public might not link the rise of fast-food restaurant chains and processed foods to enhanced food security, such links are made by proponents of recent FDI (and thus empty calorie-ization) trends. For example, "In my opinion, obesity is more the result of the success—not the failure—of the market. But on net, we are still better off" (Finkelstein and Zuckerman, 2008, p. 10), and, "We suspect that most people are better off from the technological advances of mass food preparation, even if their weight has increased" (Cutler et al., 2003, p. 116).

Whether people and societies are indeed "better off" is an empirical question that deserves closer scrutiny. The empirics, to bring us back to a point made earlier, depend in significant part on the food security yardstick used. If our yardstick is cheap—a.k.a. "empty" and "incorrectly priced" (Carolan, 2011b)—caloric availability, then I might agree with the authors of the above statements. But do calories alone a secure food system make?

Part II

Pieces missed

Chapter 3

Well-being and nutrition

"We're growing happiness." There might have been a smile on his face when he said it but I did not doubt his seriousness. It was the summer of 2011 and I was talking with a longtime friend who raises corn and soybeans. We were discussing rising commodity prices—particularly corn—and I was mentioning how volatile agrifood markets were weighing on human welfare around the world. It was at this point in the conversation when my friend said those words. Later he clarified his statement, telling me that the commodities he raises contribute directly to feeding people which ultimately makes them better off. "So the more I can grow the more happiness I generate," he proudly explained. In just a couple of sentences, this individual vocalized a widely embraced, though rarely articulated—at least not with such bluntness—assumption of current agrifood policy: that the lot of humanity will naturally improve with enhanced agricultural output. This chapter places that assumption under empirical scrutiny.

Life expectancy

I can think of nothing more fundamental to well-being than the act of living. Plainly stated, being dead puts a terrible cramp on one's welfare. In addition, food has long been understood as fundamental to life; after all, we need to eat to survive. So conventional agrifood policy, given its emphasis on caloric output, ought to enhance life expectancy—right?

I begin by looking at the relationship between life expectancy at birth and GDP per capital, as it has long been believed that economic growth is a necessary condition of food security (see e.g., Babu and Gulati, 2005). The data show the relationship between life expectancy and economic growth to be mixed. As detailed in Figure 3.1, life expectancy is strongly positively correlated to national affluence up

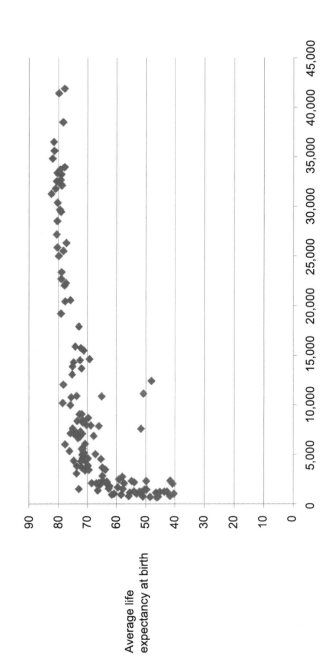

Figure 3.1 Relationship between life expectancy and GDP ($ purchasing power parity).
Source: Data obtained from FAO.

to roughly US$7,000 GDP per capita. After this point, however, the relationship noticeably begins to flatten out. And beyond US$20,000 GDP per capita, as illustrated in Figure 3.2, there ceases to be any correlation between the two variables.

The nutrition transition refers to changes in dietary patterns (namely, the consumption of more processed fats and sugars) and physical activity levels (increasingly sedentary lifestyles) that accompany a country's rising affluence and increasing urbanization. Medical innovation in disease treatment and improvements in infrastructure (such as the delivery of clean water and disposal of waste) have proven sufficient to offset the impact of these less-than-ideal diets and physical activity levels on life expectancy. Yet there appears to be change afoot, as the US looks to be the first affluent nation to have reached an unenviable tipping point. While the overall life expectancy rate in the US is holding steady (for now), a new study shows that in hundreds of counties—most located in the South—life expectancy has *fallen* in recent years. These counties also have some of the highest obesity rates in the nation, in addition to very high levels of (racial) inequality (Kulkarni et al., 2011). The study implicates the nation's food system, as diet was shown to be a major risk factor in cutting short life expectancies. The authors of the study are also quick to highlight that while some US counties are performing particularly poorly, *all* are being negatively impacted by diet and other environmental factors. In their words, the "relative [life expectancy] performance for most communities continues to drop" across the US (p. 1). I routinely hear in my travels across the US about how this particular nation's food system is the most secure in the world. Hearing this, I often mention studies like the one just highlighted and then inquire how a system responsible for cutting short average life expectancies can be held in such high esteem. I have yet to get a satisfactory response to my inquiry.

What about agricultural productivity, does it correlate positively with life expectancy? Figure 3.3 details this relationship. There is a weak relationship until around 12,000 calories per capita, keeping in mind that these calories go to feeding not only humans but also cars (as biofuels), livestock (as feed), and industry (as raw industrial inputs). Beyond this point, the relationship disappears. Yet even among countries with low per capita output levels, very high life expectancies are still recorded. We can therefore dispel the argument that productivism alone promotes life expectancy, especially once a very meager level of output is reached.

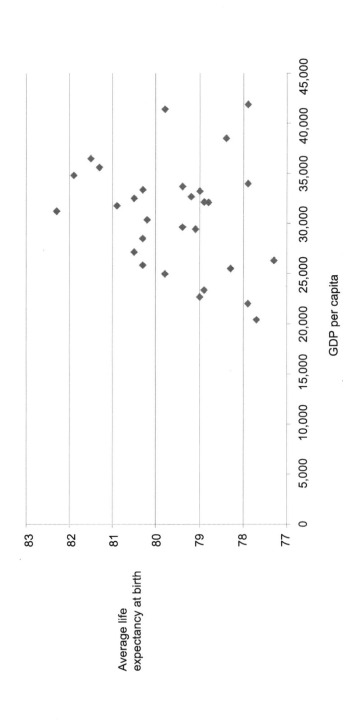

Figure 3.2 Relationship between life expectancy and countries with a GDP per capita ($ purchasing power parity) of $20,000 and greater.

Source: Data obtained from FAO.

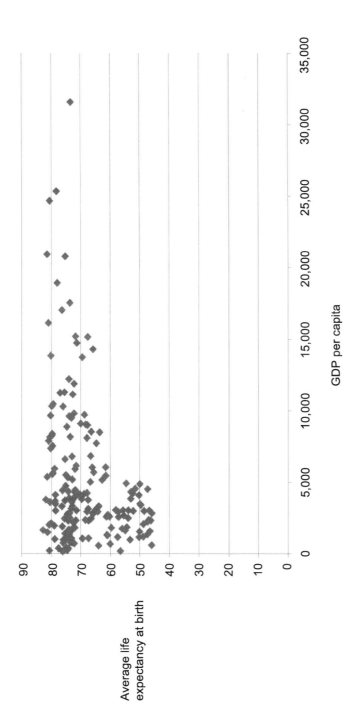

Figure 3.3 Relationship between per capita food production and life expectancy.
Source: Data obtained from FAO.

In Chapter 2, I discuss at length the pivotal role that neoliberalism has played in the conventional food security narrative. Looking at that relationship empirically, what role (if any) does a country's integration into global markets have on its average life expectancy? To answer this question I turn to data compiled jointly by the US-based think-tank the Heritage Center and the *Wall-Street Journal*, resulting in the Index of Economic Freedom. This index is a series of ten economic measurements that have been grouped into four broad categories:

1   rule of law (property rights, freedom from corruption);
2   limited government (fiscal freedom, government spending);
3   regulatory efficiency (business freedom, labor freedom, monetary freedom); and
4   open markets (trade freedom, investment freedom, financial freedom).

Countries that score 80 to 100 are considered "free," 79.9 to 70 "mostly free," 69.9 to 60 "moderately free," 59.9 to 50 "mostly un-free," and 49.9 to 40 "repressed." Figure 3.4 illustrates the scatterplot between countries' average life expectancy and their economic freedom score.

Proponents of the "neoliberalism–food security" link routinely use absolute language when advocating their cause, suggesting that returns on economic freedom never diminish. According to this logic, if some economic freedom is good, more (and more and more) must be better from a welfare-enhancing standpoint. The data seem to support their initial premise. *Some* economic freedom is better than total repression. After a point, however, the returns diminish. Looking at Figure 3.4, we can locate that threshold at a score of roughly 65. In other words, as far as average life expectancies are concerned, countries that are solidly "moderately free" perform just as well as "mostly free" and "free" countries.

Another assumption of conventional food security is that calories must be not only prevalent but cheap. The solution to the food security puzzle has thus far been to tackle issues of supply (e.g., making *more* food *cheaper*), leaving largely untouched issues of demand (e.g., improving incomes and employment opportunities for the poor) (Carolan, 2011b). Figure 3.5 plots the relationship between life expectancy at birth and the average percent of disposable household income spent on food. In some lower-incomes countries, households

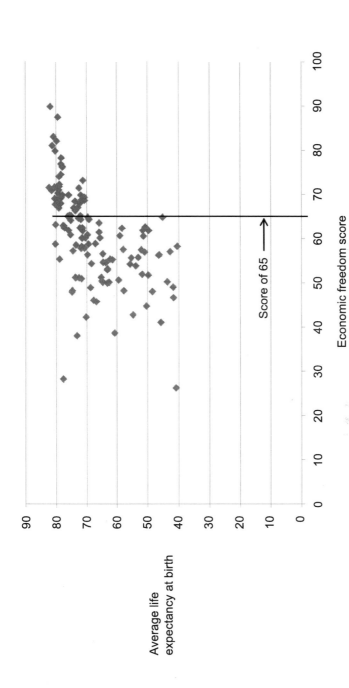

Figure 3.4 Relationship between economic freedom and life expectancy.

Source: Data obtained from FAO.

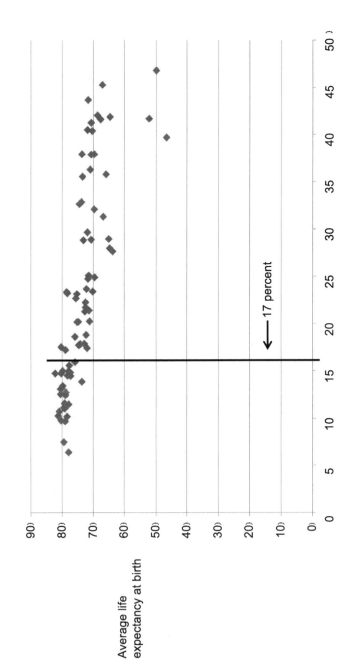

Figure 3.5 Relationship between average percent disposable household income spent on food and life expectancy.
Source: Data obtained from FAO.

can spend over 40 percent of their annual disposable income on food, while in affluent nations that figure typically falls to somewhere between 10 and 15 percent (though within the US the figure is closer to 6 percent). There is clearly nothing secure about a nation when the average household commits close to half of its disposable income to putting food on the table (and a meager amount of food it often is, at that). Yet, at least as far as life expectancies go, the returns on cheap food are diminishing. That is, until the point where roughly 17 percent of disposable household income is spent on food is reached, after which those returns disappear. And based on research mentioned earlier documenting declining life expectancies in counties in the southern US (Kulkarni et al., 2011), there is reason to believe that the link between cheap food and average life expectancies could turn *negative* once a certain level of "cheapness" is attained.

Subjective indicators of well-being

Recall the FAO's foundational principle of creating freedom from want as it applies to food and how this freedom is directed at the achievement of still deeper goals. These deeper goals, as described in Chapter 2, were first laid out by President Roosevelt in his 1941 State of the Union address when he spoke of the "four essential freedoms" necessary for human security and enhanced well-being. So, to what extent are conventional agrifood policies in keeping with the goal of making people *feel* better off (see Box 3.1)?

Box 3.1 Negative social impacts of industrialized farms

There is an extensive literature dating back to the 1940s that details numerous negative impacts that industrialized farms have upon community and individual well-being. Some of these negative impacts include the following:

1   Socioeconomic well-being:

- greater income inequality and/or higher rates of poverty;
- higher rates of unemployment; and
- reduced employment opportunities.

2   Social fabric:

- decline in local population; and
- social class structure becomes poorer (due to, for instance, increases in hired labor).

3   Social disruption:

- increases in crime rates and civil suits;
- general increase in social conflict;
- greater childbearing among teenagers;
- increased stress and social-psychological problems;
- swine concentrated animal-feeding operations (CAFOs) located in census blocks with high poverty and minority populations;
- deterioration of relationships between farming neighbors; and
- more stressful neighborly relations.

4   Deterioration in community organizations; less involvement in social life.
5   Decrease in local-level political decision-making (as outside interests gain influence).
6   Reduction in the quality of public services.
7   Decreased retail trade and fewer, less diverse retail firms.
8   Reduced enjoyment of outdoor experience (especially when living near CAFO).

(Based on review of literature by Lobao and Stofferahn, 2008, and Stofferahn, 2006)

You are not going to be very happy with life if you are starving. But equally, while conventional economic theory assumes more stuff (including food) is forever positively correlated with subjective feelings of well-being, too much of a good thing is bad from a life satisfaction standpoint. A growing body of research indicates that after a certain point more choice is associated with decreased welfare, as measured by an increased risk of depression, stress, regret, and, when it comes to food, obesity and diabetes (Jackson, 2009; Kasser, 2002; Mishan, 1967; Schor, 2005). One study looked at 7,865 female adults who were between the ages of 18 and 23 at the time of the initial survey (Ball et al., 2004). The same women were surveyed again four years later. Even after controlling for things like current occupation, young women who were overweight or obese were more dissatisfied with their careers, family relationships, partner relationships, and social activities. The authors conclude that "being overweight/obese may have a lasting effect on young women's life satisfaction and their future life aspirations" (p. 1019).

Other studies point to strong links between body mass index (BMI) and depression and anxiety, regardless of gender (Peterson et al., 2012). (BMI is calculated as weight (kg)/height (m)^2 and among adults there are four categories: underweight (less than 18.5), normal weight (18.5–24.9), overweight (25–29.9), and obese (greater than 30).) Evidence also suggests that poor diet is positively correlated with decreased life satisfaction, even after controlling for BMI. For instance, a strong positive association has been found between the consumption of soft drinks and sugary foods and suicidal behaviors among adolescents in China (Pan et al., 2011).

I turn now (briefly) to what are known as Happy Life Years. While life expectancy at birth and self-reported satisfaction surveys are indicative of how well people thrive in a country, neither captures this matter completely. One could imagine, for example, a society where people live long but not happily, such as in cases where medical technologies stretch life out well after quality life begins to diminish. Similarly, one could imagine that people live happily in a country but not for long, perhaps due to overindulgence. Combining these measures resolves some of these limitations. It is common to measure the health of nations by the average number of years people live free from chronic illness. This is often expressed in Disability Adjusted Life Years (DALYs). Happy Life Years (HLYs) are calculated to be analogous to the DALYs (see Veenhoven, 1996). HLYs = Life expectancy at birth × happiness score (on a scale of 0 to 1). For purposes of illustration, say life expectancy in Country X is 60 years. If everybody were perfectly happy (with a happiness score of 1), the average HLYs for this country would be 60. If, for example, the country's average happiness score was 0.5, the per capita HLYs lived would be 30.

Figure 3.6 examines the relationship between economic freedom (which I have already introduced) and HLYs. There are two rather striking features about this scatterplot. The first is that there is almost no correlation between the two variables. Economic freedom, in other words, appears to have very little impact on a country's HLYs.

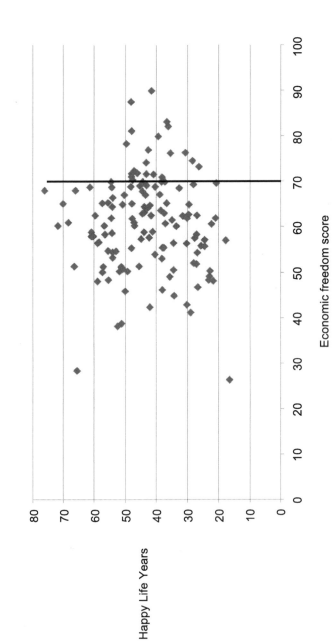

Figure 3.6 Relationship between economic freedom score and Happy Life Years.
Sources: Data obtained from the Heritage Center and New Economics Foundation.

More striking still, however, is where the two variables *do* seem to have some relationship with each other. The relationship appears to kick in at the high end of the economic freedom score and it is a *negative* one. To put it plainly, "mostly free" (70 to 79.9) and "free" (80 to 100) nations perform quite poorly in terms of their ability to generate HLYs. Not a single country with an economic freedom score of 70 or greater averages 50 HLYs or more.

Turning now to per capita food production: do increases in agricultural productivity translate into greater life satisfaction? The data, plotted in Figure 3.7, indicate that a country has a better chance of a higher life satisfaction average if it can produce at least 5,000 calories per capita. Beyond this level of productivity, however, we find gains in average life satisfaction to be negligible.

How about caloric cheapness? What is its relationship to life satisfaction? As witnessed earlier, nations with expensive food have a long way to go in terms of efficiently generating well-being in terms of average life expectancies. Yet, as also documented, at some point the returns (average life expectancy) begin to diminish and eventually disappear entirely. The same appears to hold for life satisfaction. According to Figure 3.8, the point at which returns on life satisfaction stop is when the cost of food drops below the 14 percent level. It is also worth noting how successful some countries are at generating remarkably high average levels of life satisfaction, even with relatively high food prices—note, for example, the handful of high performers in the 20 to 25 percent range. Later findings (in this chapter and beyond) will help illuminate these cases, as we learn more about some of the costs that accompany food systems that specialize in the making of cheap food (see, e.g., Carolan, 2011b).

Aggregate well-being indicators

I now turn to two widely used aggregate indicators of well-being: the Human Development Index (HDI) and the Happy Planet Index (HPI). The HDI factors in a country's life expectancy as well as measures of literacy, education, and standards of living. It was originally devised by the Pakistani economist Mahbub ul Haq and the Indian economist Amartya Sen in 1990. Its goal, in the words of Haq (1995, p. 3), is to give "human capital the attention it deserves" when talking about and implementing policies directed at the enrichment of human welfare. It is now used widely in the

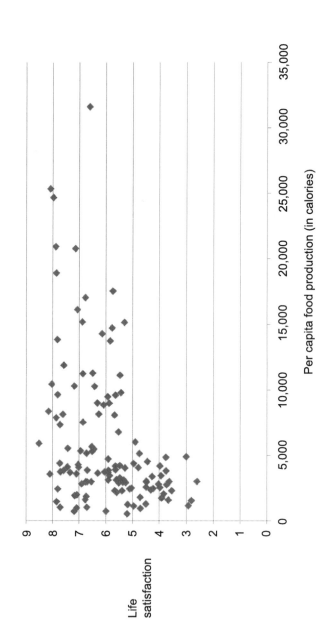

Figure 3.7 Relationship between life satisfaction and per capita food production.
Sources: Data obtained from FAO and the New Economics Foundation.

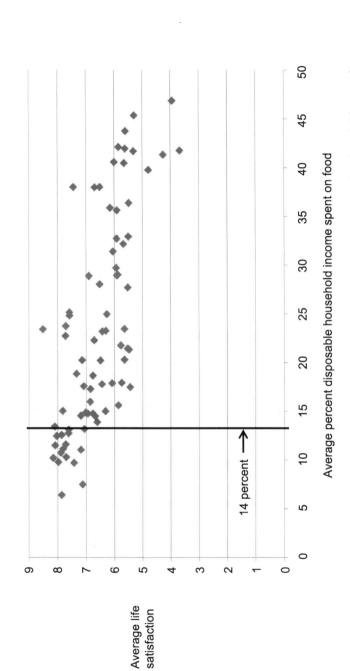

Figure 3.8 Relationship between average percent disposable household income spent on food and life satisfaction.
Source: Data obtained from FAO and the New Economics Foundation.

international development community and by organizations such as the UN.

Examining the link between HDI and GDP, we find a familiar relationship. As noted earlier with respect to other well-being indicators, beyond a certain level of affluence the generation of additional wealth has little to no positive relationship to a country's HDI score. As Figure 3.9 illustrates, after roughly US$7,000 GDP per capita returns (HDI score) on economic growth begin to drop precipitously, and they flatten out entirely after US$20,000 GDP per capita.

A similar relationship exists between economic freedom and HDI, where significant returns quickly become marginal until no returns at all are recorded. A scatterplot involving these two variables can be found in Figure 3.10. As noted earlier when assessing economic freedom's link to well-being, "free" nations appear to perform no better than nations that are "mostly free." Among "moderately free" countries, however, there is great variability in terms of HDI scores generated. Some countries in this category outperform economically "free" nations, while others have abysmal HDI scores.

As for the relationship between per capita food production and HDI scores, the story is much the same (see Figure 3.11). The two variables are strongly correlated up to around 10,000 calories per capita—though it is worth noting that the two highest HDI scores (Iceland and Norway) are from countries that produce below this level. Beyond this point the relationship between the two variables flattens out.

I turn now to the HPI. This is often misunderstood to be "just" an indicator of happiness (as, I admit, its title suggests). In reality it is an indicator of a country's ecological efficiency at producing well-being among its citizens. As stated by its authors, "the HPI is an efficiency measure: the degree to which long and happy lives (life satisfaction and life expectancy are multiplied together to calculate happy life years) are achieved per unit of environmental impact" as measured using the ecological footprint analysis (New Economics Foundation, 2009, p. 13). The HPI is based on the assumption that health (as measured by life expectancy) and a positive experience of life (as measured by life satisfaction surveys) are universal human goals whose long-term fulfillment depends on a healthy ecological base (as measured by a country's ecological footprint). The most prosperous societies, then, according to the HPI, are those that support long and happy lives without unduly costing the Earth.

HPI scores range from 0 to 100. High scores reflect a society with high life expectancy, high life satisfaction, and a low ecological

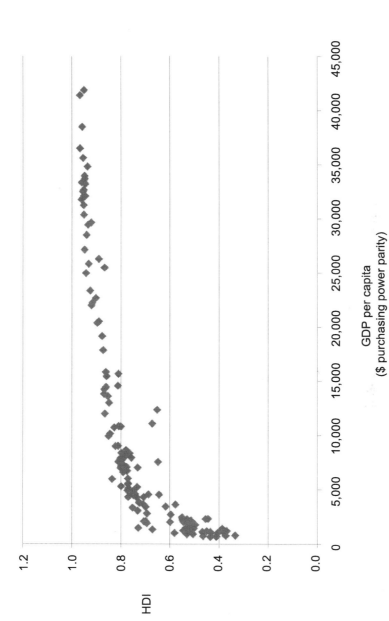

Figure 3.9 Relationship between HDI and GDP per capita ($ purchasing power parity).

Sources: Data obtained from FAO and the United Nations.

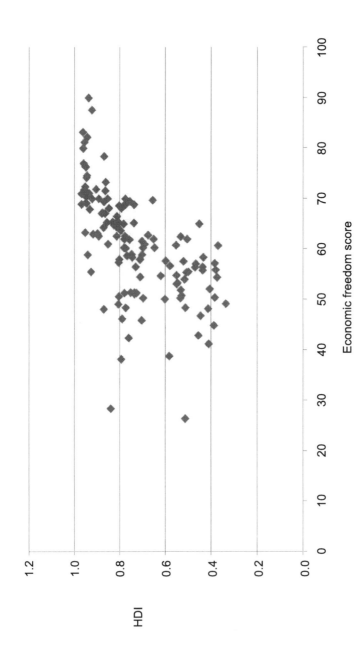

Figure 3.10 Relationship between economic freedom and HDI.
Sources: Data obtained from the Heritage Center and the United Nations.

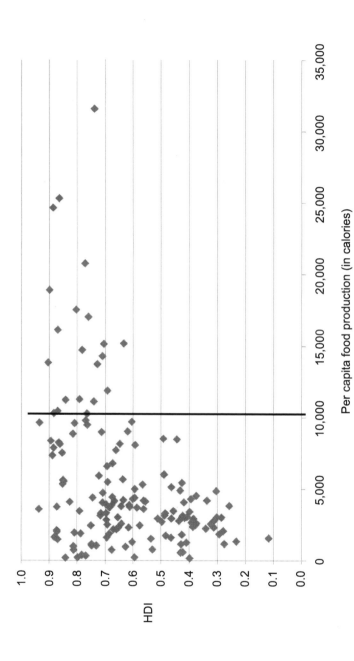

Figure 3.11 Relationship between HDI and per capita food production (in calories).

Sources: Data obtained from the United Nations and FAO.

footprint. This measure turns conventional wisdom on its head, ranking, for instance, the US in 114th place while giving the top spot to Costa Rica. Costa Ricans live slightly longer than the average citizen of the US and report having much higher levels of life satisfaction. And they do all this with an ecological footprint that is less than a quarter the size of the average person residing in the US. The HDI also supports the argument that it is not environmental throughput (a.k.a. growth) that makes a society great. Vietnam and Cameroon, for instance, have exactly the same ecological footprint: 1.3 hectares. Yet, whereas the average resident of Cameroon does not live past 50 years and reports low life satisfaction, the average Vietnamese lives as long as most Europeans (73.7 years) and reports being happier than the average South Korean (New Economics Foundation, 2009).

Plotting HPI with economic freedom reveals a troubling relationship. As Figure 3.12 illustrates, while the two variables are modestly (positively) correlated initially, the "returns" of economic freedom stop abruptly at a score of approximately 70 (the threshold between "moderately free" and "mostly free"). After this point, HPI scores plummet and never again surpass a score of 50. As far as the HPI is concerned, there really is such a thing as too much economic freedom.

Figure 3.13 examines the relationship between HPI and average percentage of disposable household income spent on food. Again we find a rather damning blow to conventional food security policy and neoliberalism more generally. As we have seen before, countries with expensive food fail to register high levels of well-being. What we have yet to see, however, is a *negative* relationship between well-being and cheap food—until now. The relationship between HPI scores and cheap food becomes regressive at roughly the point when food costs the household less than 25 percent of its annual disposable income (the dashed regression line plots this negative relationship). I suspect that this negative correlation says less about price *per se* and more about the *type* of calories that tend to be produced in nations that are able to push food prices to such low levels. I shall revisit this point shortly.

Nutritional well-being

The consumption of oils, fats, and sugars is necessary for health up to a point, after which they begin to impact health and well-being negatively (Medez and Popkin, 2004). A report by Oxford University's British Heart Foundation Health Promotion Research Group notes the deleterious effects of a high-fat (specifically animal-fat) diet. It

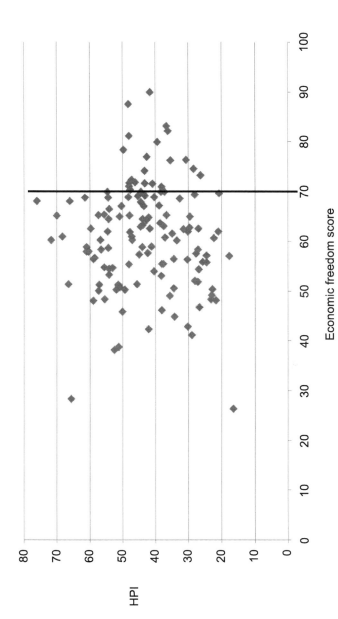

Figure 3.12 Relationship between HPI and economic freedom.

Sources: Data obtained from the Heritage Center and New Economics Foundation.

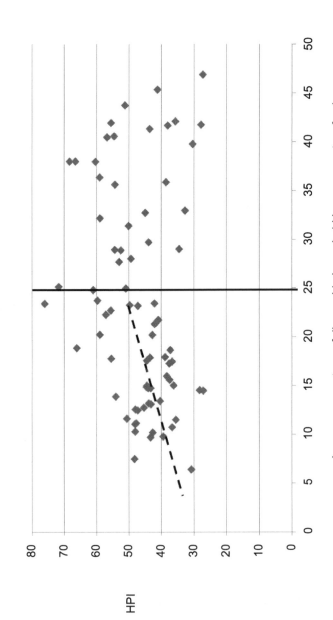

Figure 3.13 Relationship between HPI and average percentage of disposable household income spent on food.

Sources: Data obtained from the New Economics Foundation and FAO.

looked into the health implications of three diet scenarios: "current diet trends," "less meat," and "fair less meat" (Friends of the Earth, 2010). "Current diet trends" assumes a diet where the levels of meat and dairy consumed in the UK remain the same—roughly 177.7 grams (6 oz) of meat and 332.2 grams (11 oz) of milk daily. The "less meat" scenario would involve consuming 70 grams (2.5 oz) of meat and 142 grams (5 oz) of milk daily, and more fruits and vegetables. Finally, the "fair less meat" scenario assumes a fair distribution of animal protein across the UK of 31 grams (1.1 oz) of meat and 57 grams (2 oz) of milk daily, and more fruits and vegetables. A "less meat" diet was calculated to reduce UK government expenditure by £0.85 billion annually: £0.57 billion saved from reduced heart disease; £0.07 billion from reduced stroke incidents; and £0.20 billion from reduced cancer rates. More dramatic still, a "fair less meat" diet was found to save British taxpayers £1.20 billion annually: £0.80 billion, £0.10 billion, and £0.30 billion from reduced heart disease, strokes, and cancer, respectively.

As this study makes clear, a diet high in animal fat—and indeed the same applies to high-fat diets in general—comes at considerable expense to taxpayers (who shoulder the healthcare expense) as well as to the unhealthy individuals themselves (who experience decreased well-being from being sick) (see also Weber and Matthews, 2008). In sum, there are sufficient reasons for penalizing a country if the average diet of its citizenry is too calorically rich. We might even have grounds for calling that nation food insecure.

As discussed in Chapter 2, conventional agrifood policy largely does not discriminate between calories. To investigate the wisdom of this practice empirically, I will now look at the relationship between a country's daily average per capita consumption of oils, fats, and sugars and a variety of indicators. I begin by examining the link between daily average per capita consumption of oils, fats, and sugars and life satisfaction. Figure 3.14 plots this relationship. As expected, the consumption of oils, fats, and sugars at levels greater than roughly 900 calories per capita has no positive bearing on life satisfaction—in fact, beyond this point the relationship turns slightly negative.

Figure 3.15 details the relationship between daily average per capita consumption of oils, fats, and sugars and average percentage of disposable household income spent on food. Not surprisingly, as oils, fats, and sugars become cheaper—the very calories that become cheapest as food systems "modernize" (Carolan, 2011b)—we tend to consume them at greater levels (see Box 3.2).

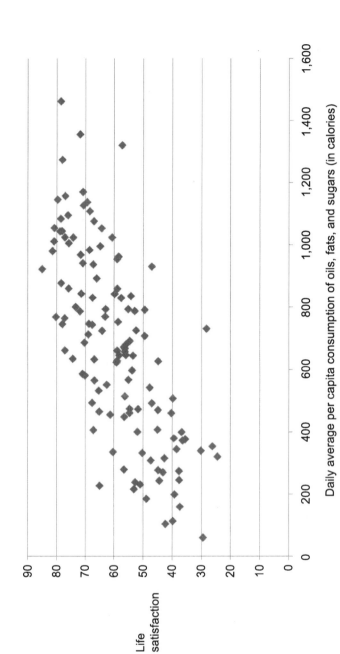

Figure 3.14 Relationship between daily average per capita consumption of oils, fats, and sugars and life satisfaction.

Sources: Data obtained from the New Economics Foundation and World Health Organization.

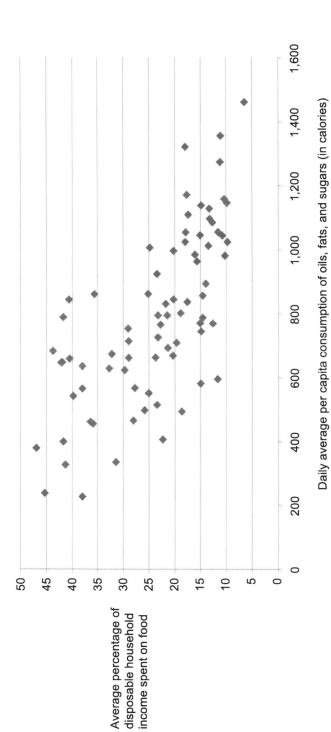

Figure 3./5 Relationship between daily average per capita consumption of oils, fats, and sugars and average percentage of disposable household income spent on food.

Sources: Data obtained from FAO and the World Health Organization.

Next, Figure 3.16 plots the relationship between daily average per capita consumption of oils, fats, and sugars and average percentage of disposable household income spent on food in countries with a GDP per capita of $15,000 or greater. This figure supports the argument, laid out previously in Chapter 2, that as countries become attractive to FDI (foreign direct investment) they undergo an empty calorie nutrition transition of sorts. Under this arrangement, nutritionally shallow foods become even more available and even less expensive. Earlier I discussed the deleterious effect of cheap food on well-being and how it is less about price *per se* and more about the *type* of calories produced in very low-cost food systems. Figure 3.16 backs up this point, as it shows a clear positive relationship between a food system's "cheapness" and an increase in the consumption of processed fats and sugars.

Box 3.2 The complicated story of quinoa

After learning about quinoa, the National Aeronautic and Space Administration (NASA) declared it the perfect food to take on long-term space exploration missions, given its complement of amino acids, fiber, vitamins, and minerals. As a centuries-old food staple in Bolivia, its dietary properties have long been known. Only in recent years, however, has the rest of the world learned about them. And now that it has learned about them, it cannot seem to get enough of quinoa. The export trade has been a boom for Bolivian quinoa growers, as their incomes have tripled over the last five years. But that also means the cost of quinoa has increased dramatically. As a result, consumption of quinoa in Bolivia has fallen by 34 percent over the same period. In its place Bolivians are eating less expensive processed foods, causing nutritionists in the country to sound alarm bells as they witness rising rates of malnutrition, obesity, and other diet-related health risks (Romero and Shahriari, 2011). Rates of obesity in Bolivia, for example, doubled between 1994 and 2003 (Pérez-Cueto et al., 2009). Concern about the country's nutritional health has reached the highest levels in the Bolivian government. In 2011, the country's president, Evo Morales, helped launch an initiative to bolster domestic production and consumption of quinoa. Packets are now being supplied to pregnant and nursing women. In addition, it is being fed at greater rates to Bolivian military personnel and to the nation's children through school lunch programs (*The Week*, 2011).

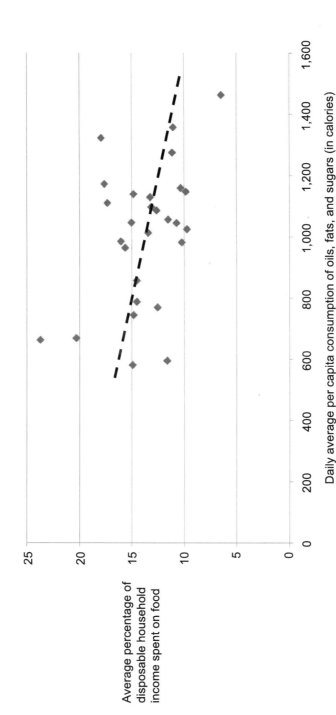

Figure 3.16 Relationship between daily average per capita consumption of oils, fats, and sugars and average percentage of disposable household income spent on food ($15,000 or greater GDP per capita).

Sources: Data obtained from FAO and the World Health Organization.

Finally, Figure 3.17 presents a scatterplot between average percentage of disposable household income spent on food and BMI "overweigh" rates for select countries (recognizing that not all countries record this data). Figure 3.17 falls in line with what we would expect to see in light of the figures preceding it. As food becomes less expensive, specifically that of the nutritiously shallow variety, we would expect a nation's average BMI to rise, which is precisely what we see in Figure 3.17. This is yet more evidence that there really is such a thing as food that is too cheap.

Before concluding this chapter, I want to say a bit more about why we need to pay closer attention to the *type* of calories being produced in very low-cost food systems. The remarkable cheapness of the average calorie in countries like the US is achieved through efficiency "gains" in the production and processing of sugars, fats, and oils— the very things we should be consuming in moderation. Take the case of the US. While claiming to have the cheapest food in the world, in reality only certain foods have become less expensive: namely, those of the highly processed variety, such as soft drinks, fats and oils, and sugars and sweets (see Figure 3.18). Conversely, the foods that public health professionals instruct us to eat more often—such as fresh fruits and vegetables—are becoming more expensive. It should come as no surprise, then, to learn that consumers are gravitating toward the lower-cost options (see Figure 3.19).

Total daily energy intake in the US increased by 300 kcal between 1985 and 2000. Refined grains accounted for just less than 50 percent of this increase, while added fats and sugars each accounted for roughly 25 percent. In contrast, the consumption of fruit increased by only 0.3 servings from the 1970s. Which fruits are consumed most? Not surprisingly, those that cost the least. Half of all fruit consumed is accounted for by six items: orange juice, bananas, apple juice, fresh apples, fresh grapes, and watermelon. Potatoes (fresh, frozen, and potato chips), canned tomatoes, and iceberg lettuce— also all low cost—accounted for 48 percent of total vegetables consumed (Drewnowski and Darmon, 2005a).

"We're growing happiness." I am afraid I cannot confirm my friend's declaration. After examining the relationship between a number of happiness and well-being indicators and phenomena said to be necessary for food security—from economic growth to per capita calorie production levels and the cheapness of food—the most I can say to affirm his statement is something we already know: people living in impoverished conditions with no food are at great

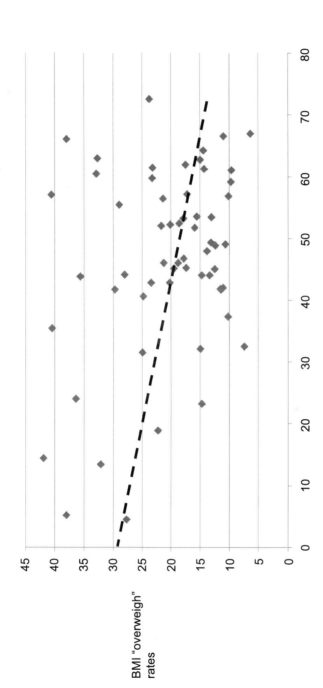

Figure 3.17 Relationship between average percentage of disposable income spent on food and BMI "over-weigh" rates for select countries.

Sources: Data obtained from FAO and the World Health Organization.

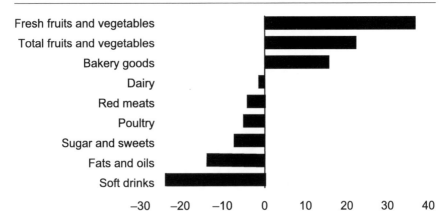

Figure 3.18 Change in food prices, 1985–2000 (converted to real 2002 US$).

Source: Adapted from Putman et al., 2002.

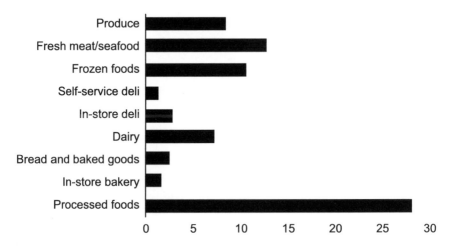

Figure 3.19 Share of supermarket sales (percentage).

Source: Based on data taken from USDA Economic Research Service, 2002.

risk of living short, miserable lives. Conventional agrifood policy has got that much right. But, as also documented, we must be careful about succumbing to the trap of absolutes. Just because having something is demonstrably better (from a welfare standpoint) than having nothing—be it economic freedom or even food itself—that does not mean we can assume that more is always better than less. For, as detailed in this chapter, that is demonstrably not the case. After a certain point, well-being returns on many of the things we have long assumed to be ends in themselves cease to be registered—or they may even turn *negative*. This ought to be reason enough to revisit the stated aims of conventional agrifood policy. But in case it is not, there are plenty more chapters to change your mind.

Chapter 4

Sustainability

"While it would be nice to put the needs of the environment first, there are a lot of people out there who need to be fed. We need to let farmers farm." I was sitting on a panel convened to discuss links between agriculture, food security, and climate change. The panelists had finished giving their assessment of the situation and were fielding questions from the audience. I did not know the individual responsible for the above statement but he clearly took issue with our making, in his words, such "a deal about long-term sustainability when people are hungry *today*." (Finding his comments so interesting, I jotted them down as accurately as I could.) I have heard similar comments before. They tend to come from individuals uncomfortable with attempts to redefine food security as being about more than just food production. That being said, I understand why some put up resistance. When you have the responsibility of "feeding the world" on your shoulders you are given considerable leeway in terms of who and what you impact.

My immediate thought, upon first hearing that person's passionate plea to combat hunger today, was "Why must we present the choice in mutually exclusive terms?" Is our option really "the environment" *or* "humans," as relayed by the individual in my story? In light of our growing knowledge in agroecology, for example, it seems instead that in order to put the food needs of humanity first we must give equal priority to the needs of the environment—after all, where is everything we need to survive going to come from if not from the Earth?

This chapter looks at the toll being placed on the environment by the respective food systems of nations. The implications of this analysis are profound. For if fundamentally unsustainable food systems are by definition food insecure, then we will need to rethink entirely the countries we seek to emulate as far as agrifood policies and practices are concerned.

Greenhouse gas emissions

Climate change poses a tremendous threat to food security. The FAO (2008) has highlighted the following populations as warranting special attention as a result of their heightened food-related vulnerabilities due to climate change:

- Low-income groups in drought- and flood-prone areas with poor food distribution infrastructure and limited access to emergency response.
- Low- to middle-income groups in flood-prone areas that may lose homes, stored food, personal possessions, and means of obtaining an adequate income.
- Farmers whose land risks becoming submerged or damaged due to sea-level rise or saltwater intrusions.
- Farmers who lack sufficient capital that would allow them to adjust to changing temperature and rainfall conditions.
- Low-income livestock keepers in dry lands where changes in rainfall patterns will affect forage availability and quality.
- Low-income livestock keepers who, due to heatwaves, will lose animals from excessive heat.
- Fishers whose infrastructure for fishing activities (e.g., port, landing, and storage facilities, fish ponds, and processing areas) becomes submerged or damaged by sea-level rise, flooding, or other extreme weather events.
- Fishing communities whose livelihoods depend on the presence of healthy coral reefs for food and protection from significant weather events.
- Fishers and aqua-farmers whose catch suffers from shifts in fish distribution and the productivity of aquatic ecosystems due to changes in ocean currents and temperatures and/or because of increased discharge of freshwater into oceans.

While climate change is particularly harmful to the world's poor (who, coincidentally, also bear the least responsibility for it), its presence will be felt by all as it impacts agricultural systems around the world. Specialized monocultures are bred to grow (and thrive) within a narrowly defined window of optimal conditions. As those conditions change the yield of "high-performance" crops will suffer terribly. Climate change also increases the risk of significant weather events that could lead to crop failures and massive unemployment among landless rural peasants whose main source of income is field labor. Areas where precipitation is expected to increase face more frequent and severe floods as well as increased erosion and reservoir sedimentation, whereas areas expecting decreases in rainfall face decreased water availability and increased droughts. Though future precipitation is notoriously difficult to predict with a high degree of certainty, models agree that increases in precipitation are mainly expected at high latitudes while decreases will be recorded in subtropical and lower-latitude regions (Rosegrant et al., 2009).

With models used in the analyses that informed the Fourth Assessment Report by the Intergovernmental Panel on Climate Change (IPCC) (IPCC, 2007), Battisti and Naylor (2009) conclude there is a greater than 90 percent chance that average growing season temperatures by this century's end will exceed any single growing season average recorded between 1900 and 2006 for most of the tropics and subtropics. These higher average temperatures are expected to increase the rate of evaporation and transpiration because of the greater water-holding capacity of the atmosphere, thus reducing water stored in reservoirs and soils. Climate change models are also in agreement that crop irrigation requirements will increase in the future, as will overall water stress in most areas dependent on irrigation (Fischer et al., 2006).

Climate change will also have a significant impact on livestock and fisheries, particularly for producers in poorer nations that lack the capital and credit to adapt to inevitable environmental changes. Climate variability will negatively impact livestock productivity due to the stress placed on rangelands and on the animals themselves. As for the impact of climate change on fisheries, this represents a perfect storm of sorts thanks to predicted increases in water temperature and oxygen demand, decreases in pH, water quality and volume, and a higher frequency of disease (Bates et al., 2008).

Agricultural systems are not only negatively impacted by climate change. They are also a major driver of it. It has been estimated that agriculture accounts for 10 to 12 percent of total global greenhouse gases (GHGs) or 60 percent of global nitrous oxide (N_2O), 50 percent of global methane (CH_4), and less than 1 percent of global carbon dioxide (CO_2) (Smith et al., 2007). (GHGs are not equal, as N_2O has roughly 300 times the global warming potential of CO_2.) If one accounts for GHG emissions from land-use changes (e.g., deforestation), agriculture may be responsible for as much as

30 percent of total global anthropogenic GHGs (Bellarby et al., 2008). Agricultural emissions increased by 17 percent from 1990 to 2005 (Smith et al., 2007). According to one life-cycle analysis, 83 percent of food-related GHG emissions for the average US household are attributable to the production sector of agriculture (Weber and Matthews, 2008).

Figure 4.1 plots the relationship between per capita food production (in calories) and agricultural GHG emissions. There is a positive relationship between these two variables. This finding should not come as a surprise, given the GHG-intensive nature of how calories tend to be produced. And I am not just talking about the emissions tied to tractors and other forms of heavy equipment. In fact, on-farm fossil-fuel consumption is responsible for a relatively small percentage of farms' GHG emissions, especially compared to the significant N_2O footprint from the production of fertilizer and methane emissions from livestock (Dyer and Desjardins, 2003). For instance, major GHG emissions associated with nitrogen-containing fertilizer production are CO_2, emitted when natural gas is combusted as part of ammonia synthesis, and N_2O, emitted during nitric acid production. One study looked at the GHG emissions savings among Canadian farmers that adopted a zero-tillage farm management practice. While zero-tillage reduces the number of cultivations and therefore cuts down the amount of fossil fuels directly consumed (as fewer passes of a field are required), it often *increases* the need for additional inputs, like fertilizers and pesticides, which have their own sizable GHG footprints. After factoring in for the life-cycle GHG emissions of these added inputs, the authors of the study discovered that they more than offset the savings by reductions in on-farm fossil-fuel consumption (Dyer and Desjardins, 2003).

What about *per capita* agricultural GHGs? When comparing countries in terms of output (of anything) it is important to factor in for population size, recognizing that looking only at overall emissions can disadvantage those with more mouths to feed. Table 4.1 lists the top twenty-five per capita agricultural GHG emitting countries. Uruguay takes the top spot, emitting more agricultural GHGs per capita than any other country (0.00887 gigagrams per person of CO_2 equivalent), followed closely by New Zealand (at 0.008425 gigagrams per person of CO_2 equivalent). The two countries take the top two spots due to their oversized methane—a major GHG of concern in both places due to their large ruminant populations—and undersized human footprints (Ulyatt and Lassey, 2001).

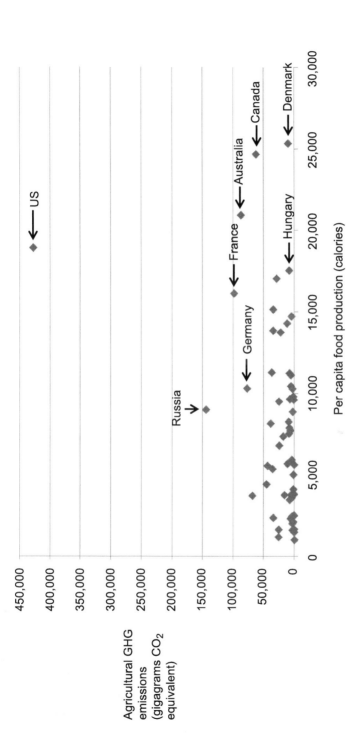

Figure 4.1 Relationship between per capita food production and agricultural GHG emissions*.

Note: * Emissions from agricultural transport and energy are excluded as these sectors are not defined as part of the agricultural sector by the IPCC (Intergovernmental Panel on Climate Change).

Source: Data obtained from FAO.

Table 4.1 Top twenty-five agricultural GHG emitting countries*

Country	Agricultural GHG emissions (gigagrams CO_2 equivalent)	Per capita agricultural GHGs (gigagrams CO_2 equivalent)
Uruguay	29322.59	0.00887
New Zealand	34826.3	0.008425
Australia	87394.74	0.004284
Ireland	17605.08	0.004233
Burundi	25917.35	0.003298
Argentina	124919.4	0.003224
Mongolia	6461.65	0.00253
Vietnam	65090.65	0.002449
Belarus	22746.95	0.002327
Brazil	415771	0.002225
Algeria	6534.62	0.002072
Denmark	10391.7	0.001919
Mauritania	5667.471	0.001913
Iceland	566.386	0.001909
Canada	58648.51	0.001815
France	98603	0.00162
Colombia	68565.58	0.001526
Lithuania	5011.962	0.001468
Luxembourg	669.076	0.001465
US	427528.5	0.001442
Madagascar	26550.1	0.001424
Bolivia	11657.17	0.00127
Romania	25444.12	0.001176
The Netherlands	18515.56	0.001135
Finland	5922.903	0.001129

Note: * Emissions from agricultural transport and energy are excluded as these sectors are not defined as part of the agricultural sector by the IPCC (Intergovernmental Panel on Climate Change).

Source: Data obtained from the FAO.

Energy consumption

Figure 4.2 plots the relationship between energy use by agriculture (in kilotonne of oil equivalent) and per capita food production (in calories). The figure reinforces the point made in Chapter 2, where I described in some detail the capital-intensive (a.k.a. *energy-intensive*) nature of the green revolution and conventional agriculture more generally. The figure should not be read as indicating that increases in agricultural productivity *must* come at the cost of heightened energy consumption. That relationship exists only as far as conventional monocultures are concerned.

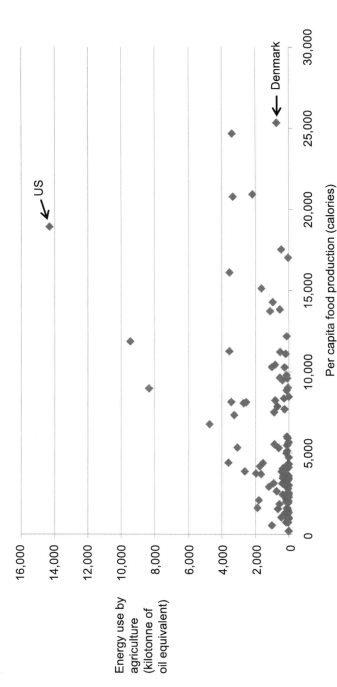

Figure 4.2 Relationship between energy use by agriculture and per capita food production*.

Note: * Energy use is indicated by the annual use of energy at the farm level and the energy used to produce mineral fertilizers for agricultural use.

Source: Data obtained from FAO.

Before we can talk about *how much* food a country can sustainably produce, we first have to determine *which* management practices are predominantly employed. We know, for example, that organic systems are more efficient from an energy input/output perspective. Take, for example, a well-managed organic corn production system that produces 8,700 kilograms per hectare (or 130 bushels per acre) in an environment like the Corn Belt of the US, where conditions are perfectly suited for this crop. Each kilogram of corn in this farm yields about 3.58 kcal of energy, or 31,132 kcal per hectare. A total of 5,377 kcal of energy is required to produce this volume of corn from a hectare, which translates to 5.8 kcal of corn energy per kcal of fossil energy invested in producing the corn. Conventional corn production systems are less efficient, yielding roughly 4.0 kcal of corn energy per kcal of fossil energy invested (Pimentel et al., 2005). In light of this, it has been calculated that if 10 percent of all corn in the US were grown organically, the nation would save roughly 200 million gallons of oil equivalent (that is 4.6 billion barrels of oil) per year (Pimentel et al., 2005).

Yet the energy savings do not stop there. While organic corn production is more labor intensive—requiring some 600,000 kcal of labor per hectare compared to conventional systems, which require closer to 462,000 kcal—that increase in labor translates into a *decrease* in soil erosion and the reduced loss of phosphorous and potassium nutrients (see also Pimentel, 2006). Granted, in this example we are talking about a situation where soil and climatic conditions are ideally suited for raising corn; conditions that are not found in every part of the world. But does that in any way nullify the aforementioned "gains" that could be achieved by rethinking how corn is raised in places like the US Corn Belt?

While fossil fuels remain the dominant source of energy within agriculture, the mix of fuels used is dependent on fertilization and cultivation practices employed. Nitrogen fertilizer is produced using large amounts of natural gas and some coal, and, according to some estimates, accounts for 50 percent of total energy use in commercial agriculture. In the UK, oil can account for between 30 and 75 percent of total energy inputs on farms, depending on the cropping system used (Woods et al., 2010). This dependency upon fossil fuels in particular is disconcerting, not only because it ties agriculture to climate change but also because it links food prices to energy prices, which are expected to remain volatile well into the foreseeable future. What's *secure* about that?

Moving beyond the farm gate, we begin to understand just how consequential diet is to shaping the overall energy footprint of a nation's food system. Unveiling the energy-intensive nature of poor diets in this manner calls into question the wisdom underlying the movement identified earlier as the empty calorie-ization of food security. While the production sector is responsible for the majority of food-related GHG emissions in affluent nations—due in large part to the CO_2 hoof-print of livestock agriculture (Weber and Matthews, 2008)—a considerable amount of energy is consumed beyond the farm gate. While the agrifood chain eats up approximately 30 percent of the world's available energy, as much as 70 percent of this is devoured by sectors other than production (FAO, 2012). Figure 4.3 provides a breakdown of where this energy is consumed in the US food system.

The takeaway message of Figure 4.3 is that bad diets are bad for the environment. The figure was constructed with the help of data from a USDA report totaling the energy used in producing, processing, and transporting food in the US (Canning et al., 2010). The final

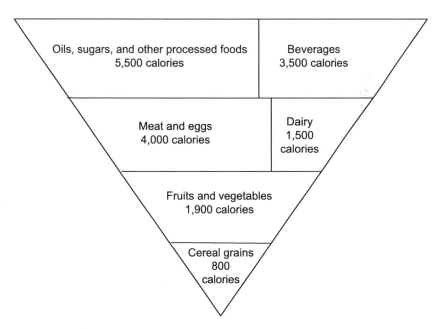

Figure 4.3 Breakdown of the amount of energy (17,000-plus calories per day per capita) consumed by the US food system.

Sources: Based on Canning et al., 2010, Carolan, 2012, and Bomford, 2011.

tally: over 17,000 calories (as a unit of energy) on a per capita daily basis. Breaking those energy units down according to specific food categories, we can see that over half go toward the making of highly processed foods; a third into the making of animal products including meat, eggs, and milk; and a sixth into grains, fruits, and vegetables. Processed foods are said to be foods that have had "value" added to them. So, as consumers, we tend to pay a little more for the added convenience: for example, pineapple that has been peeled and cored; soda packaged in a 7.5-oz (versus the standard 12-oz) can; and Oreo cookies (minus the filling) that have been crumbled for items like pie crusts. Yet, in adding value, food processers are also using energy—value added is a euphemism for *energy subtracted*. Eating well, in short, is less energy-intensive than eating poorly (Bomford, 2011).

In the previous chapter, we saw the tremendous variability between countries in terms of daily per capita consumption of oils, fats, and sugars. The US leads all countries in this respect, as the average American consumes 1,462 calories' worth of oils, fats, and sugars daily. As described in the last chapter, these calories come at great cost to public health and individual and societal levels of well-being. And we can now add the environment to that list.

Water

Rain-fed agriculture makes up just over 80 percent of all global cultivated areas and produces 60 percent of the world's food, while irrigated agriculture produces the remaining 40 percent on just 18 percent of the world's farmland (Khan and Hanjra, 2009). Fifty-three percent of cereal production growth during 2000 to 2050 is expected to be met from irrigated agriculture. Yet nearly 30 million hectares—roughly 20 percent of the world's irrigated land—have already experienced significant yield declines due to soil salinity and waterlogging (Rosegrant et al., 2009). Moreover, salinization is destroying an *additional* 1 to 2 million hectares of productive farmland annually (Khan and Hanjra, 2009). These losses must be factored in when calculating actual productivity gains made by green revolution cropping systems, as they involved crops that not only required copious amounts of water but delivery systems that could supply water at precise times during the plant's life-cycle. One estimate, for example, shows that the degradation of irrigated lands used to produce rice and wheat in the Punjab region of India reduced the gains made by breeding and infrastructural and educational investments by approximately 33 percent (Murgai et al., 2001).

Areas facing degraded water supplies are being hit with a frightening one–two punch. The first punch comes when overdrawn freshwater supplies result in land degradation (e.g., soil salinity). Then, in addition to reducing the ability of soils to maintain productivity levels, land degradation undermines its water-use efficiency (de Vries et al., 2008). In other words, these regions are seeing their freshwater sources dwindle at a time when their soils require *even more* water to grow (water-intensive) crops.

As the global demand for meat is expected to double from 2010 to 2050, the water food-print of livestock will only grow, particularly owing to the water-intensive crops (like corn, soybeans, and other coarse grains) that are fed to these animals. Depending upon the beef cow's diet in large-scale confinement operations—as the vast majority of water for industrially raised beef is consumed by irrigated pasture and feed crops—each kilogram of consumable flesh requires anywhere between 10,060 liters (Chapagain and Hoekstra, 2003) and 100,000 liters (Pimentel et al., 1997) of water. In light of all this, it is not surprising that the UN recently concluded that water scarcity—not a lack of arable land—will be the number-one constraint on food security in the decades ahead (United Nations, 2007; see Box 4.1).

Box 4.1 California water wars for the twenty-first century

On July 25, 2012, California Governor Jerry Brown unveiled plans for a US$14 billion tunnel system to divert water from Northern California to heavily populated Southern California cities and farms that grow half of the nation's fresh produce. Under the plan, two tunnels, large enough to carry up to 9,000 cubic feet of water per second, will stretch 40 miles from the Sacramento River to existing pumps and aqueducts that supply cities including Los Angeles and San Diego and irrigate 3 million acres of farmland.

Supplying water to Los Angeles has been contentious ever since the turn of last century, when more than 200 miles of aqueducts were built to supply the area (and its farms) with water. The new tunnels are designed to ease pressure on the ecologically sensitive Sacramento–San Joaquin Bay Delta, at the confluence of two rivers that feed San Francisco Bay. Pumps today draw water from the delta, killing two out of every three fish that are sucked into the system. This has pushed some species to the brink of extinction and has forced farmers to idle thousands of acres of land due to government restrictions on irrigation in a last-ditch attempt to save those endangered fish. The new tunnels will be fed using gravity to draw water under the delta.

Environmentalists oppose the project on the grounds that its impacts have not been sufficiently studied while certain farming groups refuse to pay the additional water fees associated with it and disagree with the component of the proposal that calls for restoring ecologically sensitive areas now used for agriculture.

(Marois, 2012)

There is some reason to believe that trade benefits countries that are water poor, particularly when it comes to acquiring water-intensive agricultural goods that could not be sustainably raised domestically. For example, more than 75 percent of the water pumped to the surface to irrigate wheat fields in Saudi Arabia is lost to evaporation—not a wise use of this precious resource (Myers and Kent, 2001). Nevertheless, the country went from producing virtually no wheat in 1980 to harvesting more than 4 million tons annually by the early 1990s, with massive government water subsidies for their agricultural sector (Carolan, 2011b). By substituting cereal and other food imports for irrigated agricultural production, countries can effectively reduce their agricultural water use. Importing countries benefit from such an arrangement as water originally intended for agriculture can be allocated to other uses (Rosegrant et al., 2009). A global water saving conceivably takes place when agricultural exporters are more water efficient than importers, such as when exporters produce agricultural products under rain-fed conditions while importers would have used irrigation water to produce the same agricultural commodities. One study examining the impact of trade on global water use notes that the majority of cereal exports come from countries (e.g., the US, Canada, and those in the European

Union) where grains are cultivated in a highly productive rain-fed environment (de Fraiture et al., 2004).

Yet, as discussed in Chapter 2—and I raise this point again in Chapter 5—dependency is not a long-term solution, especially when something as fundamental as food hangs in the balance. Trade's greatest benefit is also its most dangerous quality: it helps nations divorce themselves from certain domestic ecological constraints. Yet what happens when those domestic material limitations become global in character? When countries import food to overcome certain local limits they are effectively exporting those limits to their trading partners. Sooner or later, therefore, they will be facing those limitations again in the form of global market volatility unless steps toward sustainability are taken. For when limits begin to be reached, exporting countries will most certainly place their domestic food needs above those of their one-time trading partners and, quite simply, cut them off.

The subject of water food-prints is revisited in Chapter 6 when discussing the Food and Human Security Index. For the moment, let us look at the respective food-related water requirements of countries. The following data look at countries' "green," "blue," and "grey" water food-prints for domestically and internationally sourced food. The green water food-print refers to the use of water resources (such as rainwater that does not become run-off) that go toward the growing of crops. A blue water food-print denotes the utilization of water resources—surface and groundwater—along the supply chain of a product. And the grey water food-print represents the volume of freshwater required to assimilate and adequately dilute the load of pollutants that resulted from the production and processing of commodities (Hoekstra et al., 2011). Table 4.2 lists the top twenty-five water food-prints of national production (in million cubic meters of water per year). India, China, and the US make up the top three countries (in that order), each possessing a total water food-print that is at least twice the size of any other country, including even fourth-placed Brazil.

Looking only at total national water food-prints tends to disadvantage large, populous nations which by nature of their size and population consume a lot of water (China, India, and the US are the world's top three populated countries, in that order). An arguably fairer comparison would be to rank countries according to their per capita national production water food-prints. This brings us to Table 4.3, which lists the top twenty-five *per capita* water food-prints

Table 4.2 Top twenty-five water food-prints of national production (mm^3/yr)*

Country	Water food-print of crop production			Water food-print of grazing	Water food-print of animal water supply	Total
	Green	Blue	Grey	Green	Blue	
India	716004	231428	99429	42644	4707	1094212
China	623881	118941	223761	81782	9848	1058212
USA	611971	95905	118160	120996	3361	950393
Brazil	303743	8934	15917	132223	3158	463974
Russian Federation	304839	10358	11609	15447	912	343164
Indonesia	285654	11468	20778	6693	470	325062
Nigeria	190600	1087	605	5265	455	198012
Argentina	157605	4306	4958	18589	773	186230
Pakistan	40561	74272	21805	34113	907	171656
Canada	120340	1607	18165	5502	558	146171
Thailand	109585	17003	7227	5194	221	139230
Mexico	83105	13885	11382	25916	995	135283
Australia	81255	13363	7372	32240	1024	135254
Philippines	104860	3150	3717	3886	279	115892
Ukraine	98614	2573	5161	4562	378	111288
Turkey	75697	15236	9449	8158	334	108874
Iran	43027	39823	8826	13212	415	105303
Vietnam	65706	6528	9620	4425	444	86723
Malaysia	81131	1344	3001	400	71	85948
Bangladesh	62919	7825	10138	3342	434	84658
Spain	51561	14136	8292	5530	750	80269
France	62700	2849	8018	5672	778	80017
Myanmar	74939	2272	1133	650	273	79265
Ethiopia	56485	1173	327	18858	638	77481
Kazakhstan	54175	8527	387	4417	162	67668

Note: * mm^3/yr = million cubic meters of water per year.

Source: Hoekstra et al., 2011.

of national production (again in million cubic meters of water per year). The outcome of this ranking is significantly different from that contained in the previous table—China and India, for example, do not even make an appearance. At the top of this ranking is Australia. Its agricultural sector consumes the equivalent of 6,630 cubic meters of ("green," "blue," and "grey") water per person. Allow me to put that figure into some perspective. The UN argues that humans have a fundamental right to between 20 to 40 liters per person per day,

Table 4.3 Top twenty-five per capita water food-prints of national production (mm^3/yr)*

Country	Total
Australia	0.00663
Paraguay	0.00571
Argentina	0.00481
Canada	0.00452
Kazakhstan	0.00447
New Zealand	0.00403
Uruguay	0.00382
Bolivia	0.00351
Niger	0.00349
Malaysia	0.00335
Guinea-Bissau	0.00322
USA	0.00321
Mongolia	0.00314
Belarus	0.00277
Lithuania	0.00275
Belize	0.00262
Hungary	0.00257
Papua New Guinea	0.00249
Brazil	0.00248
Russian Federation	0.00240
Ukraine	0.00236
Ecuador	0.00224
Estonia	0.00223
Thailand	0.00221
Bulgaria	0.00216

Note: * mm^3/yr = million cubic meters of water per year.

Source: Hoekstra et al., 2011.

considerably more than the amount to which millions around the world presently have access (Cunha, 2009). There are 1,000 liters in one cubic meter of water. You do the math. To put it plainly: the agricultural sector in Australia uses much more than its fair share of water.

Waste

There are a lot of descriptors for a country that wastes *over one-third* of its food—"irresponsible," "unsustainable," "profligate"—but certainly not "food secure." Yet that is the reality for many of the world's most affluent nations. A recent study by the FAO reports that 33 percent of all food produced for human consumption is lost or wasted globally. That constitutes roughly 1.2 billion metric tonnes of food annually (Gustavsson et al., 2011). And the problem is getting worse.

Up to 50 percent of all food in the US is wasted, costing the American economy at least US$100 billion annually (Jones, 2005; see Box 4.2). US per capita food waste has increased by 50 percent since 1974 to more than 1,400 kcal per person per day, or 150 trillion kcal per year. Food waste generated in the US could pull approximately 200 million people out of hunger. If you were to include all the feed that went into producing the meat and dairy thrown away annually by consumers, retailers, and food services in the US and UK, the number increases to 1.5 billion people (Stuart, 2009). British consumers discard approximately 7 million tons of food—that is about a third of what they purchase. At a retail cost of around £10.2 billion (US$19.5 billion), this waste has a CO_2 equivalent of 18 million tons—an amount equal to the annual emissions of one-fifth of Britain's total car fleet (Desrochers and Shimizu, 2008). Canadians toss out about C$27 billion worth of food annually (Gooch et al., 2010). Japan's household and food industries together waste about 17 million metric tonnes of edible food each year (Venkat, 2011). In India, roughly 30 percent of the country's fruits and vegetables and 30 percent of its grain are lost due to poor storage facilities (Mukherji and Pattanayak, 2011). In China, food waste has increased exponentially in recent years and now accounts for close to 70 percent of all household and commercial waste (Xin et al., 2012). At the other extreme, some sub-Saharan African and Southeast Asian countries waste only six to eleven kilograms of edible goods per person per year (Gustavsson et al., 2011).

Box 4.2 US–Brazil biofuel trade relationship

It might seem a little harsh to talk about biofuels in the context of waste. Yet, in light of its questionable environmental benefits (Carolan, 2009), one cannot help but question the wisdom of a US policy that leads to 40 percent of a country's corn crop being devoted to ethanol production. Even more troublesome are the convoluted (and terribly wasteful) trade policies that have emerged thanks to recently implemented biofuel targets. Take, for example, biofuel trade between the US and Brazil—two ethanol superpowers. A newly published *Agricultural Outlook* from the FAO and the OECD (OECD and FAO, 2012) projects a massive rise in ethanol trade between the US and Brazil, where the US will import 4 billion gallons of ethanol from Brazil, while Brazil will import 2 billion gallons of ethanol from the US. This caused one wise policy expert to ask, "Couldn't we just save all those transactions costs and shipping-related greenhouse gas emissions by keeping our ethanol and cutting our projected ethanol imports from Brazil in half?" (Wise, 2012). The problem lies in the US biofuel mandate.

This stipulates 36 billion gallons of renewable fuel use in the US by 2022. As so-called first-generation biofuels—like ethanol derived from corn—have questionable environmental benefits, the mandate requires that the majority of this fuel must be met by "advanced biofuels." Unfortunately, production of these fuels has stalled in the US, as the country has become locked into first-generation biofuels with the help of lavish subsidies and a powerful corn lobby (Carolan, 2010). Enter Brazil, whose sugarcane-based ethanol is considered "advanced" (even though, while having a better GHG-reduction score than corn-based ethanol, sugarcane-based ethanol comes with its own social and environmental concerns). Following the most conservative of the FAO–OECD's scenarios, Brazil will import 2 billion gallons of corn ethanol from the US to make up for the domestic shortfall created by its 4 billion gallons of sugarcane ethanol exports to the US. In other words, "they'll take our low-grade corn ethanol if they can get a higher price for their sugar-based equivalent" (Wise, 2012). Not only do biofuels—especially first generation—drive up the price of food, but now we learn that they do not even help nations like the US achieve energy independence. They just make them *more* dependent on others for fuel (and food).

Figure 4.4 takes FAO food waste estimates for countries and plots them against percent of average disposable annual household income spent on food. As one would expect, as food becomes cheaper, more is wasted. There are many reasons for this (see, e.g., Stuart, 2009). One is aesthetics, or what could be referred to as the cultural expectations about how we think particular foods ought to look.

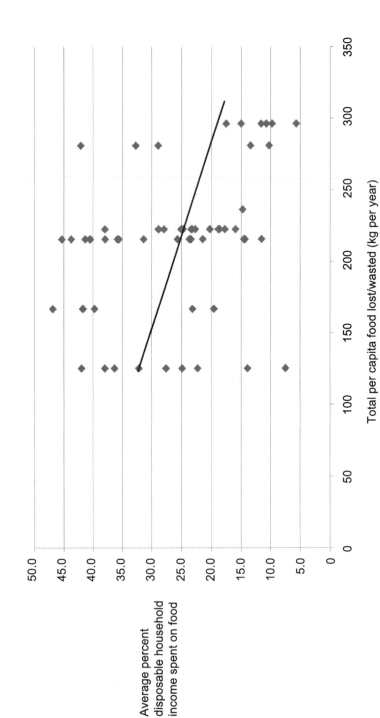

Figure 4.4 Relationship between total per capita food lost/wasted and percent of average disposable annual household income spent on food.

Source: Data obtained from FAO.

The state of Queensland, Australia, for example, discards over 100,000 tons of bananas annually because they fail to meet national cosmetic retail standards (Hurst, 2010). Globally, the bananas wasted due to failing to meet such aesthetic standards represent between 20 to 40 percent of the annual harvest (Stuart, 2009). Tristram Stuart (2009, pp. 103–111) tells a story of a British carrot grower who supplies the supermarket chain Asda. Annually, 25–30 percent of his crop fails to meet the chain's aesthetic standards. The farmer explains, "Asda insists that all carrots should be straight so the consumer can peel the full length in one easy stroke" (p. 104). Any—and only—oversized carrots go to food processors, which account for about a third of those unwanted by Asda. Small carrots require too much labor to handle so food processors usually avoid using them. Those that are left—the remaining two-thirds of the carrots rejected by Asda—are either cultivated back into the soil or fed to livestock.

The power wielded by food processors and supermarkets through market concentration also encourages food waste. Supermarkets, in particular, have considerable leverage over those "earlier" in the agrifood chain—a trend that receives much more attention in later chapters (particularly Chapter 5). This leverage comes from buyer power, which is said to exist when a market has numerous sellers but only one (or a few) buyers. Buyer power means that while supermarkets can select from a range of processors and farmers, the inverse is less the case, giving the former tremendous leverage over the latter when it comes to setting the terms of the contract. In some cases, processors and farmers supply only one supermarket chain, giving the latter tremendous leverage when it comes to dictating the terms of the contract. This allows firms like Birds Eye, for example, contractually to forbid their growers from selling their peas to anyone else, even those rejected by the company for not meeting its standards. In such a scenario growers are left with no choice but to feed their surplus to livestock or to recycle the vegetables back into the soil (Stuart, 2009). In this case, the cost of waste is pushed onto farmers.

Looking further into the FAO food waste data reveals a difference in terms of *where* food is wasted in the agrifood chain between affluent and less affluent nations. Figure 4.5 details per capita food lost/wasted at consumption and pre-consumption stages in select regions. While food is wasted and lost in every country, the amount disposed of by consumers tends to increase with

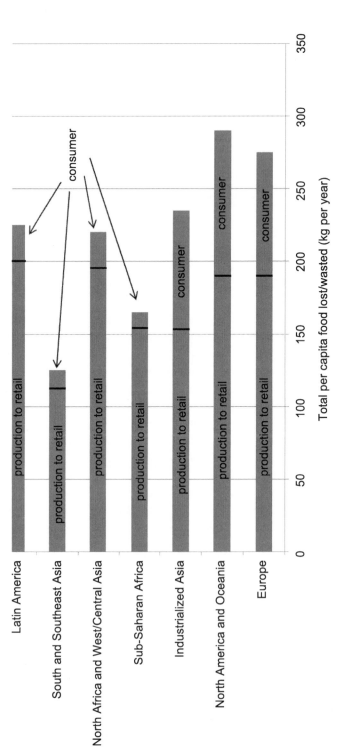

Figure 4.5 Per capita food lost/wasted, at consumption and pre-consumption stages, for select regions.
Source: Gustavsson et al., 2011.

national affluence and as average food costs decrease (Carolan, 2011b). As food becomes cheaper for households it makes simple economic sense that they will waste more of it. But this overly simplistic economic reasoning masks the unequal power relationship within food systems and therefore places too much blame on consumers (though they certainly cannot be absolved entirely for this transgression).

The aforementioned market concentration further works to super-markets' advantage by allowing them to push the cost of waste onto consumers. Take, for example, the ingenious marketing strategy by supermarkets known commonly as buy-one-get-one (BOGO) free. Grocers often reserve these campaigns for items on the brink of expiring—items they would clearly lose money on if they held on to them for a day or two longer. These schemes might be a great deal if you actually used the "free" one. The research indicates, however, that most consumers do not (Gooch et al., 2010). It is also worth noting that "sell by," "best by," and "use by" dates go largely unreg-ulated around the world. In the case of the US, for instance, the federal government regulates such dates only when they apply to infant formula. This leaves processors and supermarkets free to set their own dates for everything else. And these actors clearly have an economic incentive to make those freshness windows unduly short, which further encourages food waste.

Meat

Roughly 65 percent of all human-related nitrous oxide (N_2O) emis-sions can be traced to livestock (United Nations, 2007). Nitrous oxide has roughly 300 times the global warming potential of CO_2. When emissions from land use and land-use change are included in the calculation, the livestock sector accounts for 9 percent of CO_2 deriving from human-related activities (United Nations, 2007). It has been calculated that producing a single kilogram of beef generates as much CO_2 as driving 250 kilometers in an average European car or using a 100-watt bulb continuously for twenty days (Ogino et al., 2007, p. 424). Animal agriculture is also responsible for roughly 37 percent of all human-induced methane emissions, which has a global warming potential twenty-three times greater than that of CO_2 (United Nations, 2007).

Earlier I mentioned the rather significant water food-print of livestock, highlighting in particular the (industrial) beef cow's

Table 4.4 Feed, calories, and protein needed to produce one kilogram of chicken, pork, and beef

Grain (calories/protein in grams) ⟶	Animal (calories/protein in grams)
2kg feed grain (6,900/200)	1kg Chicken (1,090/259)
3kg feed grain (10,350/300)	1kg Pig (1,180/187)
7kg feed grain (24,150/700)*	1kg Beef cow (1,140/226)
16kg feed grain (55,200/1,600)**	1kg Beef cow (1,140/226)

Notes: * Low-range conversion ratio;
** High-range conversion ratio.

Source: Based upon data from Patnaik, 2009, and Sachs, 1999.

somewhat egregious appetite for water-intensive grains. Table 4.4 breaks down the amount of grain that goes into producing one kilogram of live weight gain for chicken, pigs, and beef cows under industrial (feed-intensive) conditions. Some animals are clearly more efficient converters of grain to animal protein than others. I discuss in Chapter 7 the place for animal agriculture (beef included) in the future that is in keeping with the understandings of food security being promoted in this book. It is not animal agriculture *per se* that concerns me, but how those animals are raised and the levels at which their protein is consumed.

If everyone in the world were to consume meat at levels comparable to that found in Luxembourg and the US—around 125–136 kg (276–300 lbs) per person per year—there would only be enough grain remaining to support a global population of about 2.6 billion people (or 38 percent of the existing population) (Roberts, 2008, p. 211). Table 4.5 takes this calculation further, estimating the global population that could be sustained if per capita meat consumption for the top twenty-five meat-consuming nations were replicated globally (assuming a beef, pork, and chicken ratio similar to that found in Luxembourg). As the table makes clear, none comes close to having a per capita meat-consumption level that could be sustainably reproduced at the global level. In other words, if we are looking for countries to emulate—at least as far as meat consumption is concerned—we are not going to find any viable candidates in Table 4.5.

Table 4.5 Top twenty-five per capita consumers of meat (and projected global population if everyone in the world consumed meat at that level)

Country	Total per person (kg)	Global population that could be supported
Luxembourg	136.5	2.5 to 3.49 billion
US	125.4	2.5 to 3.49 billion
Australia	121.2	2.5 to 3.49 billion
New Zealand	115.7	2.5 to 3.49 billion
Spain	110.2	3.5 to 4.49 billion
French Polynesia	108.9	3.5 to 4.49 billion
Austria	103.1	3.5 to 4.49 billion
Israel	99.1	3.5 to 4.49 billion
Canada	98.7	3.5 to 4.49 billion
Bahamas	98.1	3.5 to 4.49 billion
Denmark	97.8	3.5 to 4.49 billion
Kuwait	97.4	3.5 to 4.49 billion
Saint Lucia	95.4	3.5 to 4.49 billion
Ireland	94.1	3.5 to 4.49 billion
Iceland	94.0	3.5 to 4.49 billion
Portugal	92.9	3.5 to 4.49 billion
Argentina	91.7	3.5 to 4.49 billion
Italy	91.4	3.5 to 4.49 billion
France	88.7	4.5 to 5.49 billion
Malta	88.5	4.5 to 5.49 billion
Germany	87.7	4.5 to 5.49 billion
United Kingdom	85.8	4.5 to 5.49 billion
Antigua and Barbuda	85.4	4.5 to 5.49 billion
Czech Republic	85.2	4.5 to 5.49 billion
Slovenia	83.8	4.5 to 5.49 billion

Source: Data obtained from FAO.

Environmental Performance Index: agriculture

The 2010 Environmental Performance Index (EPI), developed by the Yale Center for Environmental Law and Policy, ranks 163 countries on 25 performance indicators tracked across 10 well-established policy categories covering both environmental public health and ecosystem vitality (Emerson et al., 2010). One of the "policy categories" evaluated by the EPI is agriculture. Three indicators go into measuring countries' performance in this area.

- *Agricultural water intensity*. This represents a measure of sustainability (for reasons already discussed), arrived at by calculating water withdrawn for irrigation and livestock purposes as a percent of total available water resources.

- *Agricultural subsidies.* Government subsidies for agricultural production and agrochemical inputs intensify environmental pressures by encouraging energy-intensive management practices, farm-scale increases, and the expansion of agriculture into ecologically sensitive areas (Key and Roberts, 2007). This indicator measures subsidies as a proportion of agricultural value.

- *Pesticide regulation.* Pesticides represent a significant risk to the health of the public as well as the environment, particularly given the levels at which they are being found in some freshwater supplies. One study estimates that the annual costs of pesticides in drinking water for the US, UK, and Germany are US$1,126,337,798, US$287,444,066, and US$180,522,199, respectively (Leach and Mumford, 2008). In another analysis, looking just at the US, this cost was placed at US$2 billion per year (Pimentel, 2005; see also Table 4.6). In still another study, after totaling the costs of pesticides, nitrate, phosphate, and cryptosporidium (protozoan pathogen), agriculture's toll on freshwater sources in the UK was calculated at US$515 million annually (Pretty et al., 2005). The pesticide regulation indicator of the EPI tracks government attention to the issue (as the tracking of pesticide use across countries is uneven), including, for example, participation in various international conventions directed at the regulation and/or elimination of hazardous chemicals.

Figure 4.6 plots the relationship between agriculture EPI scores and GDP per capita. There are a number of striking features about this figure. Perhaps most notable is that it dispels the myth perpetuated by free-market enthusiasts that economic growth is unequivocally good for the environment. As argued by the Property and Environmental Research Center (the oldest pro-free-market and private-property institute in the US): "Market forces also cause economic growth, which in turn leads to environmental improvements. Put simply, poor people are willing to sacrifice clean water and air, healthy forests, and wildlife habitat for economic growth" (Anderson, 2004). Figure 4.6 supports neither the claim that "poor people" are bad for environmental quality—indeed, a number of relatively poor nations (e.g., Panama) have perfect scores!—nor the

Table 4.6 Estimates of the real costs of pesticides (US$)

Costs	UK	US	Germany
(Adapted from Leach and Mumford, 2008)			
Pesticides in sources of drinking water	287,444,066	1,126,337,798	180,522,199
Pollution incidents, fish deaths, and monitoring costs	20,360,620	161,720,798	51,355,453
Biodiversity/wildlife losses	29,942,089	207,383,142	6,224,903
Cultural, landscape, tourism, etc.	118,570,678	insufficient data	insufficient data
Bee colony losses	2,395,367	144,597,420	1,556,225
Acute effects of pesticides to human health	2,395,367	167,428,591	28,012,065
Total	461,108,190	1,807,467,750	267,670,848
(Adapted from Pimentel, 2005)			
Public health impacts	not calculated	1,140,000,000	not calculated
Domestic animal deaths and contaminations	not calculated	30,000,000	not calculated
Cost of pesticide resistance and loss of natural enemies	not calculated	2,020,000,000	not calculated
Honey-bee and pollination losses	not calculated	334,000,000	not calculated
Crop losses	not calculated	1,391,000,000	not calculated
Bird and fishery losses	not calculated	2,260,000,000	not calculated
Groundwater contamination	not calculated	2,000,000,000	not calculated
Government regulations to prevent damage	not calculated	470,000,000	not calculated
Total	not calculated	9,645,000,000	not calculated

Sources: Leach and Mumford, 2008, and Pimentel, 2005.

argument that more economic growth is always better from the perspective of sustainability. While EPI agriculture scores show a moderate positive relationship with growth early on, we can see that the relationship flattens out after US$10,000 GDP per capita. More striking still is what happens after US$30,000 GDP per capita: the relationship turns *negative* (correlation coefficient of –0.59).

Like other figures before it, Figure 4.6 challenges a number of long-held assumptions about economic growth and its relationship to sustainability and food security more generally. In addition to

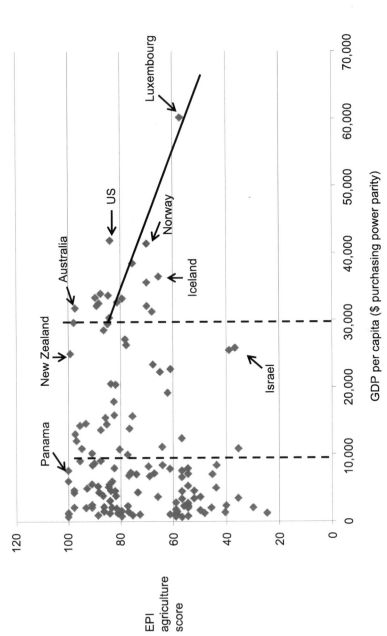

Figure 4.6 Relationship between EPI agriculture score and GDP per capita (\$ purchasing power parity).

Sources: Data obtained from Yale Center for Environmental Law and Policy and FAO.

being neither sufficient nor necessary for the higher aim of (sustainable) food security, Figure 4.6 suggests that economic growth is *detrimental* to this quest after a certain level of affluence is reached. To put this another way: Figure 4.6 reminds us that economic growth can turn *uneconomic* in character, referring to the point at which it occurs at the *expense* of systems (natural, social, etc.) that are fundamental to its very existence. And the same looks to hold true for current policies and practices directed at food security, realizing that after some point they begin to promote a type of *unsecure* food security.

Chapter 5

Food sovereignty, safety, and access

The term "food sovereignty" has received considerable attention in recent years; so much so that in March 2012 the FAO agreed to introduce it formally into its public deliberations. The reason for its ascendency—though, as mentioned at the beginning of the first chapter, it is still not well known outside agrifood policy circles—is due in large part to the perceived (and real) politicization of the term "food security" in recent decades as it has become appropriated by neoliberalism (Lawrence and McMichael, 2012). When discussed in the context of a movement, food sovereignty is deeply infused with sentiments that prioritize democratic control over national food policy and local choice for both producers and consumers. In this chapter, I have a much more conventional understanding of the term in mind, in that I liken sovereignty to choice. Rather than seeing food choices enhanced, many (if not all) affluent nations have witnessed a choice erosion, which is the direct result of market concentration in the input, processing, and retail sectors of agrifood commodity chains (Carolan, 2011b). So, in addition to everything else discussed up to this point, I would like to add choice to the list. Genuine food security can occur only when producers and consumers are given more of it, not less.

Choice also lies at the heart of food (and food worker) safety. Agrifood chains have become highly specialized in the quest for cost advantages achieved through what are known as economies of scale. But specialized systems are also highly susceptible to disruption, for by definition they lack the redundancies and diversities that lie at the heart of more resilient systems. (Biologically diverse systems are more resilient than monocultures for the same reason.) As the organizational form of "modern" food systems moves from a diverse to a specialized arrangement—to one lacking, in a word, choice—I worry about the unnecessary risks to which humans around the world are being exposed. This is not to say that agrifood chains in food secure nations ought to be risk free. But they ought to be flexible enough to ensure the safety of laborers while keeping local disturbances from turning into regional- or national-level consumer tragedies.

Farmer dependency

I have already described some of the difficulties of being a small-scale producer in a less affluent nation, but conditions are not much better for farmers in places like Australia, Canada, New Zealand, and the US. Farming is a sector unlike any other. Treating it otherwise, for reasons I will explain momentarily, has proven disastrous for producers—an ill-advised outcome for any nation looking to enhance its food security. Market concentration in the heart of the agrifood chain has been allowed to occur under the guise of "economies of scale" and "market efficiencies" (*dis*economies of scale and market *in*efficiencies are more apt descriptors). These structural changes have locked producers into an unequal relationship with their suppliers and buyers. For example, farm-gate prices for cereals, after making adjustments for inflation, have either remained steady or declined over the last eighty years. Meanwhile, the price of inputs has increased, on average, more than sevenfold (unlike most other sectors, farmers sell their products at wholesale price but pay retail for their inputs).

When looked at from gene to grocery bag—that is, from the input sector all the way through to the consumer—the population of the agrifood chain takes on an hourglass figure that is precariously hanging by a thread. Beyond the input sector, which is dominated by a handful of global giants, we find a system with significant producer and consumer populations. The hourglass shape reflects the highly truncated "middle," where food processors and manufacturers and food and beverage retailers reside. Figure 5.1 superimposes the agrifood chains of the US and New Zealand (minus food wholesaler numbers for New Zealand as the data were not available). While this shape reflects what has become of agrifood chains in affluent nations, it is also a sign of what is to come for lower-income countries as they follow in the food-prints of their more affluent neighbors.

So why does this matter and how does it negatively impact farmers? Two terms come immediately to mind: monopoly and monopsony. Most people are familiar with the former—after all, many of us grew up playing the popular board game that is its namesake. Monopoly refers to a concentration among sellers to the point at which they, rather than the market, get to set the price of the commodities they

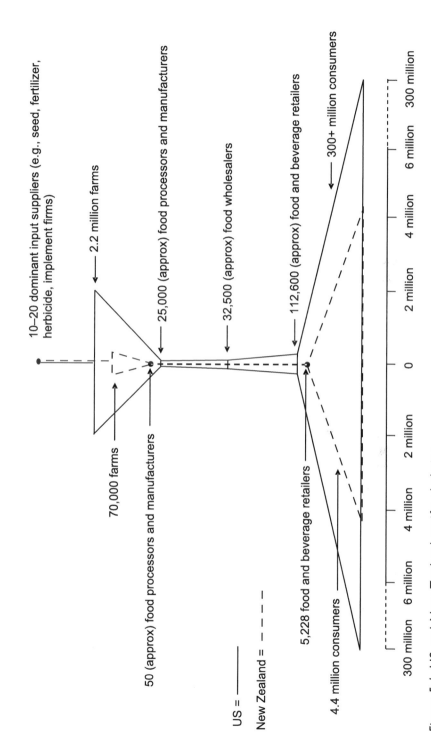

Figure 5.1 US and New Zealand agrifood chains.

are selling. Monopoly, in other words, is a statement of seller power. Yet there is also buyer power, which is where monopsony comes into the picture. This is when market concentration has reduced the number of potential buyers to the point that the seller (e.g., a farmer) has few options but to accept the price dictated by whoever is looking to purchase their goods.

A popular measure of market concentration is the four-firm concentration ratio—or simply CR4. The CR4 is defined as the sum of market shares of the top four firms for a given industry. A standard rule of thumb is that when the CR4 reaches 20 percent a market is considered concentrated, 40 percent is highly concentrated, and anything past 60 percent indicates a significantly distorted market. With this in mind, note in Table 5.1 the level of concentration in select US agricultural markets.

As already indicated, the input sector is particularly concentrated. Moreover, as most conventional inputs are owned/controlled by transnational firms, this concentration is global in character. For instance, in 2008 the CR4 for proprietary seed sales at the global level was 53 percent (ETC, 2008)—though recent acquisitions no doubt place the CR4 figure today at closer to 60 percent. Or take potash and phosphorous production: two firms control 70 percent of the global trade of these two fertilizers (Blas, 2010).

Turning now to Monsanto, a firm that securely holds the lead in terms of annual sales among seed firms (see Figure 5.2). Between the

Table 5.1 Concentration of select US agricultural markets.

Sector	CR4*
Beef Packers	83.5%
Soybean Crushing	80.0%
Steer and Heifer Slaughter	79.0%
Pork Packers	67.0%
Broilers	58.5%
Turkeys	55.0%
Pork Producers	37.3%
Ethanol Production	31.5%
Corn Seed	CR1 80.0%
Soybean Seed	CR1 93.0%
GE Cotton Seed	CR1 96.0%

Note: * Unless otherwise stated.

Sources: Developed from Domina and Taylor, 2010, Hendrickson and Heffernan, 2007, Paarlberg, 2010, p. 130, and Wise, 2010.

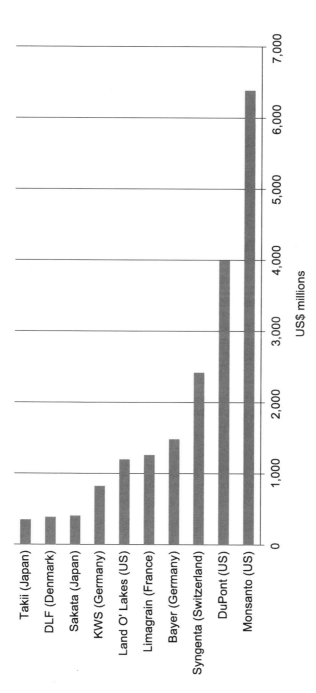

Figure 5.2 Annual sales for world's top ten seed companies.
Source: ETC Group (http://www.etcgroup.org/en).

late 1980s and late 1990s the company spent close to US$9 billion accumulating new biotech and seed companies. Today, its market dominance in so-called green (agriculture-related) biotechnology is unmatched (see Howard, 2009), as evidenced by the fact that seed and licensed traits (including those licensed to other companies) that they own now provide between 80 and 90 percent of the firm's gross profits.

Monsanto is using its extensive patent portfolio to develop cross-licensing agreements with other agribusinesses, thereby allowing it to consolidate its grip on the industry. Other firms need access to Monsanto's extensive list of proprietary technology, which explains the firm's extensive agreements with each of the other major patent-holding firms (see Figure 5.3). An example of what can come of such an arrangement is SmartStax. Jointly owned by Monsanto and Dow,

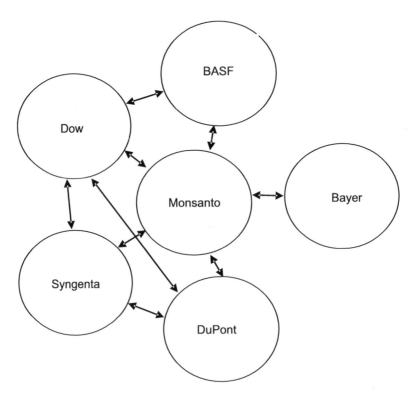

Figure 5.3 Cross-licensing agreements for patented traits among the top six patent-holding firms (as of 2008).

Source: Based on Howard, 2009.

SmartStax is a seed genetically engineered to give protection against above- and below-ground insects. It is also herbicide tolerant.

Farmers are therefore impacted by supra-competitive (monopoly) prices *charged* by input suppliers and are being squeezed accordingly. But they are also being pinched at the other end, except here it is because of sub-competitive (monopsony) prices *paid* by buyers. The very nature of farming makes it highly susceptible to buyer power. For one thing, many of the commodities farmers produce are perishable. Livestock producers cannot wait for a better price, as they need to sell their animals at optimum weight—a window that may close after just a week or two. In the case of hogs, a timely sale is also essential in order to make room for the next litter. For dairy producers, the bulk tank must be emptied daily, making it impossible for the farmer to hold out for a better price. It is also very difficult for livestock producers to vote with their feet by seeking out competitive distant markets when those closer to home are dominated by one or two buyers. Unlike processors, whose products travel well (e.g., frozen beef patties), producers do not have the luxury of being able to ship their animals great distances. Shipping live animals can be prohibitively expensive, increase animal mortality and carcass shrinkage, and result in a drop in the quality of their meat (which will negatively affect the price the farmers receive).

Agriculture is also different from sectors further along the agrifood chain in that farmers and ranchers have little ability to control or reduce capacity when markets are flooded. While processors can reduce shifts or even temporarily close one of their plants, farmers cannot make their crops come in slower or reduce the gestation period of their animals. Processors therefore can be said to have more capacity to manipulate the flow of commodities through their sector than producers. This represents yet another case of how the former possess greater market power than the latter (Domina and Taylor, 2009).

Once established, buyer power can have an amplifying effect on market inequalities, creating a type of "waterbed effect" (Foer, 2010; Inderset and Valletti, 2011). This occurs when a buyer is able to demand below-market prices from suppliers, giving that firm a significant competitive advantage over its competition. At the same time, those suppliers (especially the larger ones), in an attempt to recoup their losses, sell their commodities to other buyers (especially the smaller ones) at inflated prices. This *further* disadvantages small processors relative to those large enough to exert buyer power, thus hastening their demise and their likely acquisition by the firms exerting buyer power.

Another important component in this is the rise of contract farming. In livestock production, where contracts are most widely utilized, the contractor (the processing firm) owns the animals, while also typically supplying feed, veterinary services, and transportation when the time comes for the animals to be slaughtered. Producers, conversely, are responsible for building and managing the facilities (which are always to the contractor's specifications). While this might sound equitable, the aforementioned concentration means that while processors have their pick of producers, farmers may have only one or two firms from whom to obtain a contract. This leads to a situation where the producer lacks "exit power"—the power to walk away from negotiations in search of greener (more profitable) pastures. Given this asymmetry in negotiating power, contracts also often place the vast majority of risk on producers. Poultry farmers can invest as much as a million dollars in facilities that have a twenty–thirty-year economic life with no practical alternative use. Therefore, once a facility is built, the producer is under tremendous pressure to obtain and maintain their contract with processors, no matter how unfairly it might be structured. A medium-sized finishing hog operation with six 1,100-head hog houses costs, on average, between US$600,000 and US$900,000 to build. Between 1995 and 2009, poultry growers in the state of Alabama, USA, saw a *negative* net return in ten of those fifteen years, which averaged out to a total loss of more than US$180,000 per farmer (Taylor and Domina, 2010).

Though this concentration is said to benefit consumers, there is little evidence to suggest that it actually does. The only actors that this concentration clearly benefits are those firms exerting market power. The following statistics reflect changes in inflation-adjusted farm value and retail price for select food groups from 1967 to 2009 in the US (Domina and Taylor, 2009).

- Processed fruits and vegetables: retail price increased 6 percent while farm value decreased 24 percent.
- Fats and oils: retail price decreased 13 percent while farm value decreased 49 percent.
- Cereals and bakery products: retail price increased 14 percent while farm value decreased 57 percent.
- Dairy products: retail price decreased 12 percent while farm value decreased 61 percent.

When producers are squeezed by market power, income is siphoned out of rural agricultural areas and moved to corporate financial centers (Domina and Taylor, 2009). This is the result of a decrease not only in farm incomes but in rural incomes across the board, as processors (and the remaining large-scale producers) also have buyer power in terms of purchasing rural labor. In other words, as the countryside is gutted of its farmers and smaller processors, those that remain find a standing reserve of employment at their beck and call, which depresses rural wages. Take, for example, the weekly earnings for animal slaughter-plant workers in the US (including overtime and adjusted for inflation, in 2009 US$). In 1984 the figure was US$700. In 2010 those earnings had dropped to US$475 (Domina and Taylor, 2009).

Market concentration creates massive market inefficiencies as it distorts prices while locking certain actors into dependent relationships with their buyers and suppliers. Highly concentrated agrifood chains therefore undermine a country's food security, as this dependency restricts choice and flexibility—conditions essential for any resilient food system to take root (Almas and Campbell, 2012). So is there any way to rank countries in the aggregate in terms of their respective levels of farmer dependency? I will now attempt to do this by way of a proxy variable, as I know of no direct measure.

Table 5.2 lists the top twenty-five countries in terms of their share of total land area devoted to organic agriculture. Countries that did not make the list, for some points of comparison, include the United Kingdom, with 4.1 percent devoted to organic agriculture (27th place); France, with 2.3 percent (37th place); New Zealand, with 1.1 percent (49th place); the US, with 0.48 percent (64th place); and Japan, with 0.19 percent (93rd place). Conventional producers have to rely upon input suppliers for their seed and agrichemicals, particularly those planting, for example, herbicide-tolerant seed, which requires the purchase of a specific chemical brand. "In contrast," as noted in a recent report from the Department of Agricultural Economics at the University of Missouri, "because the organic producer does not rely on any farm chemical input . . . [they are] relatively less dependent than the conventional and GM farmers" (Harvey et al., 2012, p. 13).

Though admittedly an imperfect indicator of farmer sovereignty, there are reasons for linking organic production to greater farmer choice and national food independence more generally. Take, for example, the case of Cuba. The collapse of the Soviet Union in 1991 left the country in a rather precarious position. Not only did it mean

Table 5.2 Top twenty-five countries in terms of
share of total land devoted to organic agriculture

Country	%
Falkland Islands	35.7
Austria	16.4
Liechtenstein	15.5
Samoa	14.5
Sweden	12.7
French Guiana	11.5
Estonia	10.4
Czech Republic	8.9
Latvia	8.7
Italy	8.3
Slovakia	7.5
Switzerland	7.4
Finland	7.4
Timor-Leste	6.7
Dominican Republic	6.5
São Tomé and Príncipe	6.4
Uruguay	6.3
Slovenia	6.3
Portugal	5.7
Denmark	5.6
Germany	5.6
Norway	5.6
Vanuatu	4.8
Spain	4.8
Lithuania	4.8

Source: Data from FAO.

the loss of a major trading partner but the Soviet Union was also
Cuba's main supplier of fertilizers, pesticides, petroleum, and grain
(Warwick, 2001). Losing the Soviet Union thus proved disastrous not
only for Cuban farmers but for the population as a whole as it left the
country unable to feed itself for the first time since the revolution in
1959 (Perfecto et al., 2009). While capital-intensive agriculture had
helped feed the nation, it also made it heavily dependent upon (and
thus vulnerable to) outside forces that were beyond anyone's control.
If Cuba wanted to feed itself, it either needed to reestablish trading
partners quickly or switch to a model of agriculture that was less
input dependent (thus making the country as a whole less dependent
upon other firms and nations for its food). And so began the process
of integrating scientific and traditional knowledge to make Cuba
more food independent through organic agriculture (Perfecto et al.,

2009, p. 65). This transition has been so successful that in 1999 the Grupo de Agricultura Organica (GAO), a Cuban organic farming association that has been at the forefront of the country's transition from industrial to organic agriculture, was awarded the prestigious Right Livelihood Award (also known as the Alternative Nobel Prize).

This is not to suggest that organic producers cannot get locked into dependent relationships. As sellers, for example, organic producers are still subject to buyer power. But not being beholden to others for necessary inputs is, I would argue, better than if one were structurally in the position to be victimized by *both* buyer *and* seller power. As in the case of Cuba, national food security is also enhanced when domestic agrifood chains retain a certain level of national food sovereignty.

The issue of input independence in particular will only grow in salience in the years ahead as essential resources become increasingly scarce. And I am not just talking about inputs like water and oil. Phosphate, for example, which is essential for plant growth, is being consumed at wholly unsustainable rates. If current trends continue, the world will exhaust its supply by the early twenty-second century (likely much sooner) (Carolan, 2011b). Well before that happens, however, the world's phosphate exporters (China and Morocco hold almost 75 percent of global reserves) will have cut the rest of the world off from this precious resource to secure reserves for domestic consumption. Other countries would do well to wean themselves from this imported commodity now, before it is too late.

Constricting consumer choice

Figure 5.4 depicts sales in three sectors of the food system—the input industry, food processors and traders, and retail—during 2004, 2006, and 2012. The overall size of the "pie" has increased by roughly 50 percent during this period. Yet even more remarkable is the growth in the retail sector, where sales have more than doubled. At the same time, sales in the input and processing sectors, while growing in absolute terms, have seen their respective "slices" (as percentages of the total pie) shrink. The retail sector has emerged as *the* dominant sector in agrifood chains today in many countries. At the time of writing, Walmart was on track to generate US$444 billion in sales 2012—that is 12.3 times greater than the projected 2012 sales of McDonald's (at US$36 billion) and 33 times greater than the projected 2012 sales of Monsanto (at US$13.5 billion) (Walmart, 2012; McDonald's, 2012; Barr, 2012).

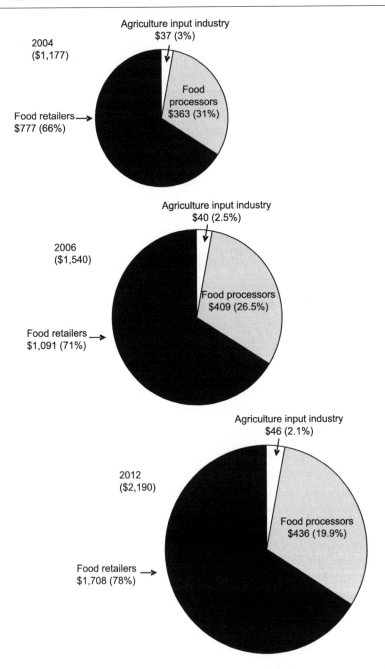

Figure 5.4 Sales of top ten companies for three sectors of the global food system (in US$ billions).

Sources: Data from Braun, 2007, p. 4, Planet Retail (http://www1.planetretail.net), and Smith, 2012.

The power of processors lies largely in their ability to manipulate prices as buyers. As sellers, however, in light of the aforementioned growing dominance of the retail sector, they too become victims of buyer power. Yet they still have the power to redistribute these "costs" onto farmers, which allows them to remain highly profitable. For example, US-based Smithfield Foods is the world's largest pork producer and processor with annual revenue in excess of US$10 billion. Even so, it would never dare try to overcharge Walmart for its pork. As the largest single global purchaser of pork products, Walmart holds considerable buyer power over Smithfield Foods. General Mills and Kraft Foods, for instance, each generate roughly one-fifth of their revenue through Walmart retail sales (Bloomberg, 2009). When such a large chunk of a firm's revenue comes from a single contract, the buyer in this relationship has significant negotiating power.

The retail sector is further consolidating its power thanks to the establishment and growing popularity of "private labels"—also known as in-store brands. Some scholars have gone as far as to argue that, with the exception of a very few select iconic brands (like Coca-Cola), "the primacy within the food system of long-standing, mass-produced branded food lines is coming to an end" (Burch and Lawrence, 2007, p. 102). Sales in private labels are growing almost twice as fast as sales of branded products. It is expected that private-label sales among the world's top thirty grocers will increase by 40 percent (to US$209 billion) by 2014, accounting for 24.1 percent of total grocery sales (Toops, 2011). Private labels are sourced from a variety of suppliers, including the very companies (such as Heinz and Unilever) whose brands will be competing with these less expensive alternatives. Manufacturers have learned that it is better to compete against a private label that they have manufactured than against a private label made by a rival. Then there are slotting fees: a pay-to-play (and then pay-to-stay) arrangement where food manufacturers pay grocers not only to stock their products but to stock them in a prominent (eye-level) place. Slotting fees can cost as much as US$40,000 per item per store (Shimp, 2009). For new products, they have been known to exceed the prod- uct's sales revenue for the first year (Hauter, 2009, p. 41). For example, slotting fees in the US paid by manufacturers have been estimated to amount to approximately US$10 billion annually (Burch and Lawrence, 2007). There is also evidence linking concentration in the grocery sector with higher retail prices (see, e.g., Anders, 2008; Dimitri et al., 2003). A study of the UK market estimates that recent retail mergers have increased grocery prices by roughly 7 percent (Cotterill, 2006).

Table 5.3 lists the top twenty-five countries in terms of super-market concentration. Globally, market concentration in the food retail sector varies considerably between nations. For example, independent grocers still represent 85 percent of retail sales in Vietnam and 77 percent in India (von Braun, 2007). Compare this to countries like Australia and New Zealand, each with a CR5 statistic of 99 (and a CR2 statistic close to 80) (Wardle and Baranovic, 2009).

Supermarkets are known to provide local growers with an important market for their products in both developed and developing countries (see, e.g., Moustier et al., 2010; Reardon et al., 2003). Yet as this sector undergoes concentration those markets become increasingly difficult to access for small-scale producers. Take Walmart's announcement in 2008 when it committed to source more local produce. Yet the retail giant gets its "local" food from a handful of very large farms—not

Table 5.3 Top twenty-five countries in terms of supermarket concentration

Country	CR5
Australia	99
New Zealand	99
Finland	91
Norway	91
Sweden	91
Switzerland	85
Ireland	83
Slovenia	83
Denmark	82
Iceland	81
Estonia	80
Ghana	80
Lithuania	77
Austria	75
Canada	75
Colombia	75
France	71
Germany	71
United Kingdom	71
The Netherlands	70
Portugal	69
Spain	68
Hungary	60
US	60
Brazil	58

Source: Data from Planet Retail (http://www1.planetretail.net).

exactly the suppliers most people have in mind when they think about "supporting local growers." The reason for this boils down to—you guessed it—economics. Only large farms can afford (or have access to sufficient credit allowing them to afford) the "minimum" requirements demanded by Walmart, such as UPC barcode technology, US$2 million in commercial liability insurance, and a financial stability rating (Adams and Salois, 2010). Moreover, given Walmart's sheer size, it makes a lot more economic sense to obtain its products from a handful of very large producers (or maybe even one) than thousands of small-scale farmers. For instance, Walmart buys over a billion pounds of beef every year to supply US consumers (Food and Water Watch, 2012). That is the equivalent of more than 2.2 million beef cows. To meet that demand with small-scale producers Walmart would have to enlist an army of feeders and ranchers. The transaction costs involved in coordinating such an effort would be near herculean. And even if Walmart did find enough small-scale producers to meet their needs, those feeders and ranchers would certainly not be able to afford the firm's technology requirements for managing inventory—costs, I should add, that Walmart *could* bear but do not because of their buyer power. I mention all of this not to absolve Walmart but to point out what happens when retail markets come to be dominated by a powerful few.

Food safety

There is also an irreconcilable tension between efficiency and safety, which I think we ought to be mindful of when thinking through what it means to be food secure. At some point the pursuit of the former comes at the detriment of the latter. While production efficiencies and scales of economy make food today remarkably inexpensive in some parts of the world, these market-based "gains" also presuppose an organizational form that is *inherently* risky from the standpoint of public health. Take, for example, slaughter facilities. Mistakes will inevitably happen as they continue to increase their speed and improve their efficiency. Ever-increasing production-line speeds increase the risk of cutting open internal organs during the evisceration process, exposing meat to fecal matter and dangerous bacteria. Moreover, thanks to market concentration, the meat from one contaminated carcass now gets mixed with that from thousands of other animals. In the past, those bacteria would have remained confined to one animal's meat. Now they can constitute a *nationwide* food threat (see Box 5.1).

Box 5.1 The USDA's new poultry rules

The USDA (at the time of writing: late summer, 2012) is set to implement new rules for poultry processing, increasing the maximum line speed at chicken plants from 140 to 175 birds a minute. It also recently announced that it will cut many of its Food Safety Inspection Service (FSIS) inspectors. These individuals examine chickens for blemishes, defects, and contaminants like fecal matter. Although one inspector would remain on the line, private plants would become primarily responsible for inspecting chickens. Together, it is estimated that these changes will save the government US$90 million annually. But it is not just about saving money. The USDA also claims that these steps will *improve* food safety. That is because the remaining FSIS inspectors will spend more time on what the USDA considers the greatest cause of food-borne illnesses: pathogens (e.g., salmonella and campylobacter). Since these cannot be detected by a visual examination, the inspectors will focus on ensuring that plants are following the proper sanitation and antimicrobial programs, rather than, say, looking for fecal matter on the birds themselves. Besides, whoever is left on the line to inspect the birds visually will not likely find much, considering that they will have about a third of a second to examine each chicken carcass.

The claim that these measures actually improve food safety is clearly questionable. Yet they undeniably undermine safety in one crucial respect: worker safety. The widespread dangers faced by poultry workers are well documented—from lost fingers to musculoskeletal disorders like carpal tunnel syndrome and tendinitis. Compounding the problem is the fact that many poultry-plant employees are immigrants and refugees, many of whom are undocumented—a population unlikely to complain about working conditions. Advocates for line workers, such as the Southern Poverty Law Center (which handles many poultry-worker legal cases), argue that existing line speeds are already too fast (Jamieson, 2012). For them, measures that increase line speed by 25 percent are simply inhumane from a worker standpoint. Yet inhumane policies are what we risk establishing when we choose to define food security around narrowly focused ends like calories and cost.

The status quo is also responsible for putting at risk millions of people who are tasked with feeding us. Van Der Hoek and colleagues (1998) estimate that approximately 7.5 percent of agricultural workers in Sri Lanka experience occupational pesticide poisoning every year. In Costa Rica and Nicaragua, the corresponding figures are 4.5 and 6.3 percent, respectively (Wesseling et al., 1993; Garming and Waibel, 2009). In one study in the West African country of Benin, 81 percent of pineapple farmers and 43 percent of vegetable farmers reported "considerable" negative health effects due to pesticide exposure (and only 1 percent reported zero negative effects) (Williamson, 2005).

CAFOs (concentrated animal-feeding operations) are another well-studied area from the standpoint of worker and public health. Work in animal agricultural industries ranks among the most hazardous of all occupations (Mitloehner and Schenker, 2007). A review of the literature published in 2007 found seventy peer-reviewed studies documenting the adverse health effects linked to working in a CAFO environment (Donham et al., 2007). Many worker injuries can be attributed to accidents with machinery and animals (Miller et al., 2004), but chronic diseases due to environmental contaminants are also posing a considerable risk to workers (Mitloehner and Schenker, 2007). According to the aforementioned literature review, over 25 percent of CAFO workers suffer from respiratory diseases, ranging from bronchitis to mucous membrane irritation, asthma, and acute respiratory distress syndrome (Donham et al., 2007). While public health professionals have set the maximum recommended prevalence of dust in livestock buildings at 2.5mg per cubic meter (Donham, 2010), studies have found it frequently reaches 10–15mg in CAFOs during cold weather (when buildings are closed up and ventilation is low) or when animals are moved (a practice that kicks up a lot of dust) (Mitloehner and Calvo, 2008).

Another issue of concern involves the use of antibiotics in the raising of livestock. There is nothing in a cow's evolutionary past quite like a feedlot. The main course in these spaces is corn, a diet that makes the cow's stomach, which normally has a neutral pH, abnormally acidic. When left untreated, acidosis can kill the animal. Antibiotics help treat the symptoms long enough for the animal to be "finished"—that is, brought up to slaughter weight. A handful of countries have banned growth-promotion use of antibiotics, such as Denmark and Germany. At the other end of the spectrum is the US.

An estimated 70 percent of all antibiotics used in the US go towards maintaining healthy livestock (Union of Concerned Scientists, 2008). Non-therapeutic use of antibiotics accounts for 90 percent of all anti-biotics used in the US livestock industry in the form of low-level feed additives (Donham and Thelin, 2006). When the subject of banning hormones is brought up, those in support of the practice immediately turn the subject back to food security: without them, they contend, it will take longer to bring cattle to slaughter weight and meat prices will rise. Yet this reflects an incredibly narrow (and dangerous) understanding of food security—again, a narrow interpretation that centers on calories and cost.

Livestock have been identified as the most likely sources of drug-resistant strains of such microbes as salmonella and campylobacter. The former sickens tens of thousands of people annually in the US alone. The latter's impact is even greater, causing more than 2 million illnesses, 13,000 hospitalizations, and over 100 deaths each year in the US (Scott et al., 2009). The drug-resistant *E. coli* strains found on poultry and beef from grocery stores and the strains in sick patients have been found to be genetically identical (Eckholm, 2010). But it is not just about meat. We now have evidence that antibiotics from the livestock industry are ending up in organic vegetables. Researchers from the University of Minnesota (Kumar et al., 2005) planted green onions and cabbage in manure-treated soil. After six weeks, cutting about 2.5cm above the soil surface, the tops of the crops were removed and analyzed. The cuttings contained traces of chlortetracycline, a widely used antibiotic among pig producers. In another experiment, conducted by the same research team, corn, green onions, and cabbage were planted in soil treated with liquid hog manure. The harvested plants were all found to contain low levels of antibiotics.

For another example of how our blind devotion to economies of scale and market efficiencies undermine food security, take the highly publicized Starlink corn debacle that occurred in the US in 2000. Approved two years earlier for livestock consumption only, Starlink corn was genetically engineered to produce a protein that is toxic to European corn borers (and other insects), thereby minimizing the need for pesticides. The protein represents a potential food allergen for humans, which is why it has not been approved for human consumption. Starlink corn was grown on less than 1 percent of the total US acreage in 2000 (approximately 362,000 acres, or 146,500 hectares).

Contamination was first noticed in September 2000, when a lab identified the protein in a sample of Taco Bell taco shells. This triggered a massive recall involving approximately 300 food products (including over 70 types of corn chips and 80 different kinds of taco shells), while 500 million bushels of corn were destroyed due to commingling in grain elevators. To limit further contamination, the USDA (in late September) bought back corn suspected of being contaminated directly from farmers. Yet there was still the issue of what to do with the previous year's Starlink crop, which had already been delivered to local grain elevators. In October, an agreement was reached between Arventis—the company that held the patent on Starlink corn—and the attorneys general from thirteen states to extend compensation to local grain elevators holding the previous year's crop (Lin et al., 2002). In the end, US$3 billion was spent containing the contamination, and even then Arventis company officials admitted it was impossible to remove all traces of Starlink from the corn supply due to the structure of the agrifood chain in the US (Hishaw, 2007).

The last point about food safety I would like to touch on involves the issue of food-borne illness. There are approximately 76 million cases of food-borne illness a year in the US (Weise, 2010; see also Box 5.2). That is a morbidity rate of 24,516 food-related illnesses per 100,000 of the population. Australia does not perform any better, averaging 5.4 million food-borne illnesses a year—or 24,545 cases per 100,000 of the population (OzFoodNet, 2010). Or take Greece, which averages 37,000 food-borne illnesses annually per 100,000 of the population (Gkogka et al., 2011). Let me put these figures into some perspective. Davao City, in the Philippines, has an illness (morbidity) rate for diarrhea of 2,143 cases per 100,000 of the population among 0–5-year-olds and 3,979 cases per 100,000 of the population among all ages. How can a country be called "food secure" when it has a food-borne illness rate *ten times greater* than a developing country's illness rate for diarrhea (the GDP per capita of the Philippines is US$2,223)? And things look to be getting worse, at least in the US. Illnesses stemming from infections from campylobacter, salmonella, and listeria *increased* in the period 2008–2011, as compared to the period 2006–2008 (GAO, 2012).

Box 5.2 Infectious animal diseases

Dozens of zoonotic disease threats have emerged in recent years *because of* current agrifood policies and practices. Some of the more famous include the H5N1 virus—a.k.a. severe acute respiratory syndrome (a.k.a. SARS)—which infected thousands and killed hundreds, and the H1N1 virus—a.k.a. swine flu—which infected tens of millions and killed over 10,000 (CDC, 2010). While animal–human transfer of infectious agents has been occurring ever since animals were first domesticated, what we are seeing today is unprecedented in terms not only of the frequency of transfer but the virulency. The reason for this, according to the world's foremost expert on avian influenza, Robert Webster, is that "farming practices have changed." He goes on to explain that today

> we put millions of chickens into a chicken factory next door to a pig factory, and this virus has the opportunity to get into one of these chicken factories and make billions and billions of these mutations continuously. And so what we've changed is the way we raise animals and our interaction with those animals. And so the virus is changing in those animals and now finding its way back out of those animals into the wild birds.
> (Council on Foreign Relations, 2005)

Compounding matters further is how we shuttle animals around the world; again, as detailed in Chapter 2, all in the name of food security (see, e.g., Ilbery, 2012). Modern animal transport systems are particularly well suited for spreading disease. Animals from different herds or flocks are confined together for long periods of time in poorly ventilated environments, giving micro-organisms and viruses every opportunity to move across the resident population. In one study, two samples—a hide swab and a fecal sample—were collected from 200 steers and heifers from a large (65,000-head-capacity) feedlot prior to and after shipping to a commercial packing facility. Levels of salmonella on hides and feces increased dramatically during transport—from 6 to 89 percent and from 18 to 46 percent of the total population, respectively (Barham et al., 2002).

How can systems that create (and spread) highly virulent diseases claim to be simultaneously enhancing food security?

Import dependency

As indicated earlier, the world's smallholder farmers are under attack. Traditional farming is viewed as unnecessarily labor intensive (never mind that conventional agriculture is unnecessarily capital- (or more specifically *energy-*) intensive). Dismantling peasant agriculture, so the argument goes, would free up literally hundreds of millions of people to work in factories, as there are roughly 1.2 billion peasants in the world today (van der Ploeg, 2008). Cities: that is where real wealth is generated. But structural changes in agriculture have occurred at breakneck speed compared to the snail's pace of other sectors, leaving hundreds of millions dispossessed, unemployed, and hungry. For example, while Mexico gained jobs in the manufacturing sector thanks to the North American Free Trade Agreement (NAFTA), employment gains have been outpaced by losses in agriculture, which saw its total employment numbers drop from 8.1 million in the 1990s to 5.8 million in the second quarter of 2008 (Zepeda et al., 2008). As for those who remain in agriculture, they are told they need to produce more with less labor, which can be achieved only with the help of technology, inputs, and fossil fuels.

Non-farming sectors of developing economies have rarely grown fast enough to absorb the surplus labor "freed from the shackles of unremitting toil on the land" (Ellis, 2005, p. 144). This strategy of constantly squeezing the farming sector has made countries *more* food insecure, not less, as it makes them economically fragile and heavily dependent upon major grain-exporting nations. Three of every four poor people in developing countries live in rural areas, which explains why public investments in agriculture in poor countries, in the forms of research and extension, yield higher societal returns than expenditures in other productive sectors of the economy (Fan et al., 2000; Bezemer and Headey, 2008). As discussed in Chapter 2, a thriving (labor-intensive) agricultural sector is essential in lower-income economies as rural poverty is the underlying cause of most cases of household food insecurity in these parts of the world. But we also know that a thriving domestic agricultural sector provides another benefit as far as food security is concerned: food independence.

Take the case of Haiti. Before 1986 the country produced much of its own food, including rice. Its agricultural sector was protected through tariffs, but these were eliminated as a result of trade liberalization. Shortly thereafter the market became flooded with cheap rice imports from the US. In 1985, Haiti imported 7,000 metric tonnes of rice; in 2004, that figure had grown to 225,000. These cheap imports did make food more affordable for the urban poor, for a time. Estimates by the World Bank (2002) indicate that the real price of rice to consumers was reduced by about 50 percent after trade liberalization in Haiti. Yet is food security achieved through policies directed at supply alone—that is, is cheap food an end in itself? What about demand? If people are not earning an income, what good is cheap food to them? Lest we forget: cheap food is often built on the backs of people undercompensated for their labor—like the German supermarket that was found to be selling inexpensive fruit by contracting with farms in Latin America that were paying their workers US$0.75 an hour (Lang et al., 2009).

Moreover, countries dependent on food imports place themselves at the mercy of global markets. Yet these markets have proven incredibly volatile, so cheap food is rarely cheap for long when coming from global markets—something Haitians experienced first hand. Prior to the food crisis of 2008 (when food prices spiked around the world), roughly one-half of Haiti's hard currency was used to purchase food. At the height of the crisis, though, poor urban households found the price of food had exceeded 100 percent of their disposable income. Having placed all of its eggs in the global market basket, the Haitian government had no choice but to accept these higher prices. The move to gut their domestic agricultural sector to enhance national food security proved disastrous. In fact, it had precisely the opposite effect.

Countries dependent on food imports also place themselves at the mercy of exporting countries. For example, 80 percent of all rice exports in 2010 came from Thailand, Vietnam, India, Pakistan, and the US. In that same year, 85 percent of wheat exports came from only four regions—namely, North America, Russia, Europe, and Australia—while 81 percent of corn exports originated from North America and South America (largely Argentina and Brazil) (Agarwal, 2011). Yet what happens when these exporting countries decide, for example, to shift large quantities of grain to biofuels? Obviously, such a move would (and has) cut into food grains available in the global market, leaving import-dependent nations in quite a bind. Similarly, concentrating export production within a few regions means that adverse weather conditions in one part of the world threaten the food security of nations located halfway around the globe.

There are a variety of ways to calculate and rank a country's level of dependency upon global markets for meeting its domestic food needs. One measure is known as the import dependency ratio (IDR). Calculated by the FAO, the IDR = imports/(production + imports − exports) × 100. Table 5.4 lists the top fifty countries in terms of their IDR. One item that immediately stands out is that it is not solely

Table 5.4 Top fifty countries in terms of import dependency ratio.

Country	Ratio
Singapore	213.5642
The Netherlands	164.6111
United Arab Emirates	143.3724
Belgium	127.6645
Slovenia	127.0207
Mauritius	109.9046
Bahrain	104.9823
Kuwait	100.0654
Netherlands Antilles	99.64059
Bermuda	98.70997
Djibouti	98.46832
Malta	98.28267
Barbados	97.25642
Jordan	94.85136
Saint Vincent and the Grenadines	94.4505
Seychelles	94.02396
Maldives	93.83737
Bahamas	90.68862
Brunei Darussalam	89.6767
Trinidad and Tobago	89.3347
Fiji	88.58428
Antigua and Barbuda	88.11378
Saudi Arabia	87.69644
Cape Verde	84.80401
Cyprus	83.7865
Yemen	82.85044
Libyan Arab Jamahiriya	80.14553
Israel	80.07225
New Caledonia	79.9685
Occupied Palestinian Territory	79.84145
Luxembourg	79.08857
Iceland	77.8771
Botswana	77.19151
Lebanon	76.62294
Portugal	76.11135
Montenegro	75.26242
Serbia	75.26242
Saint Lucia	74.20426
Lesotho	71.92938
Latvia	71.89576

(*Continued overleaf*)

Table 5.4 Continued

Country	Ratio
Mauritania	71.36757
Iraq	70.46993
Republic of Korea	68.61315
Japan	67.59718
Jamaica	67.20015
Grenada	66.95007
Georgia	65.12338
Ireland	64.59661
Algeria	61.3391
Norway	59.66622

Source: Data from FAO.

low-income countries that are dependent upon the international market for their food. Many affluent countries are, too. To put these ratios in perspective—especially those exceeding 100—note the ratios of some countries that did not make it into the top fifty: Sweden, 37.628 (93rd place); France, 23.753 (121st place); Canada, 22.337 (135th place); and the US, 6.402 (195th place).

Some countries, admittedly, are facing geographic and demographic realities that are largely beyond their control. For example, they may lack ecological resources (e.g., arable land) and/or have too large a population to be able to rely entirely on domestic production for meeting their food needs—Singapore, the Netherlands, and United Arab Emirates are cases in point. Nevertheless, if we can agree that food sovereignty and independence actually enhance food security, by giving nations flexibility and choice, then we ought to reward those countries that have it.

Part III

Looking forward

Chapter 6

The Food and Human Security Index

A lot of terrain has been covered and a considerable amount of data presented. Yet I know from many years in the classroom that a "data dump" can sometimes have the opposite intended effect as audiences risk losing sight of the larger argument. It is a common problem too for books seeking to take a big-picture view; after all, it is hard to remain focused on the forest when all you talk about are trees. A lot of trees were covered in the previous three chapters, so readers might be forgiven for losing sight of the food security forest. This chapter seeks to refocus discussion back onto the big picture of food security.

I do this with the help of the Food and Human Security Index (FHSI). The FHSI, which was first introduced in a special issue on food security of the *International Journal of Sociology of Agriculture and Food* (Carolan, 2012), was developed to challenge conventional understandings of food security. Following the original spirit of the concept, the term "human" is included in the index's title as a conceptual reminder that human welfare enhancement should be the ultimate goal of any food system (which, I should add, presupposes ecological sustainability, otherwise the entire house of cards comes crashing down). This macro-level index, which has been calculated for 126 countries, looks at a collection of indicators from the previous three chapters—of individual and societal well-being, ecological sustainability, food dependency, nutritional well-being, and agrifood market concentration. The FHSI is composed of national-level data for five indicator variables:

- *Life expectancy at birth*: indicator of individual and societal well-being.
- *Life satisfaction*: indicator of individual and societal well-being.

- *Total per capita water food-print as a percentage of total per capita renewable freshwater supply*: indicator of ecological sustainability and potential for food independence.
- *Daily per capita consumption of oils, fats, and sugars*: indicator of individual and societal well-being, ecological sustainability, and nutritional well-being.
- *Supermarket concentration*: indicator of freedom in agrifood chain.

It is not my intention to suggest that quantitative macro-level indicators are the only—or even the best—way to measure food security levels across countries. Whether we like it or not, however, metrics matter. And what we measure affects what we do. Choosing not to think outside the food security box will only result in more of the same, which, while effective at enhancing global caloric output, has undermined many of the things that make our lives healthier, longer, happier, more sustainable, and, ultimately, more secure. The remainder of the chapter is devoted to (re)introducing each indicator used in the FHSI and describing its relevance to food and human security.

Individual and societal well-being

Recall that the FAO's foundational principle of creating a "freedom from want" as it applies to food is modeled after Roosevelt's "four essential freedoms," which were introduced in his 1941 State of the Union address. The deeper goal of these freedoms is human security and enhanced well-being. In keeping with its original spirit, genuine food security must enhance well-being. The FHSI includes objective and subject measures directed toward this end. The objective measure is a country's average life expectancy at birth. As I have already discussed, there is a rich literature documenting the links between food availability, accessibility, and affordability and individual and societal levels of health—at least up to a certain level, after which overconsumption can have a negative effect on life expectancies (Medez and Popkin, 2004; Monteverde et al., 2010). The literature is quite clear: well-being generated through a country's caloric affluence has a ceiling. After this is reached, increases in per capita calorie consumption begin pulling down health indicators. As the epicentre of cheap calories, we are beginning to witness the effects of this in the US. As noted in Chapter 3, while the overall life expectancy rate in the US holds steady, it is falling in hundreds of counties throughout the South, due to high obesity rates and other diet-related illnesses (Kulkarni et al., 2011). This provides some context for the mixed relationship between life expectancy and economic growth highlighted previously. To recall from Chapter 3, life expectancy was shown to be strongly positively correlated to national affluence up to roughly US$7,000 GDP per capita. After this point, the relationship starts to flatten out. And beyond US$20,000 GDP per capita, there ceases to be any correlation between the two variables.

The FHSI also includes the following subjective well-being indicator: average reported levels of life satisfaction for each country (on a scale from 0 to 100). Clearly, life satisfaction is not going to be high when people are starving. But equally, while conventional economic theory assumes increased consumption (including consumption of food) is forever positively correlated with welfare, too much of a good thing, as has been made clear in earlier chapters, can negatively impact life satisfaction (Mishan, 1967; Kasser, 2002; Jackson, 2009). As with life expectancy, the relationship between life satisfaction and economic growth is varied, especially among countries with a GDP per capita greater than US$10,000 (see Figure 6.1). One particularly striking aspect of Figure 6.1 is how some countries are able to produce high levels of life satisfaction among their citizens with a fraction of the wealth found in other countries. For example, the average Costa Rican reports being considerably more satisfied than the average citizen of the US even though the former has *one-fourth* of the latter's wealth.

Ecological sustainability

Conventional understandings of food security are remarkably silent on the subject of sustainability. From a long-term food security perspective, however, large ecological footprints are fundamentally unsustainable and therefore ought to be avoided. We know, for example, that diets consisting of large amounts of highly processed foods come at tremendous cost to the environment, as "value added" processing consumes significant amounts of energy, water, and other natural resources (Carolan, 2011b). The same holds for diets high in animal fats/protein. The greater the per capita consumption of animal flesh (especially beef), the greater the diet's ecological footprint (D'Silva and Webster, 2010). It seems impossible to define a nation

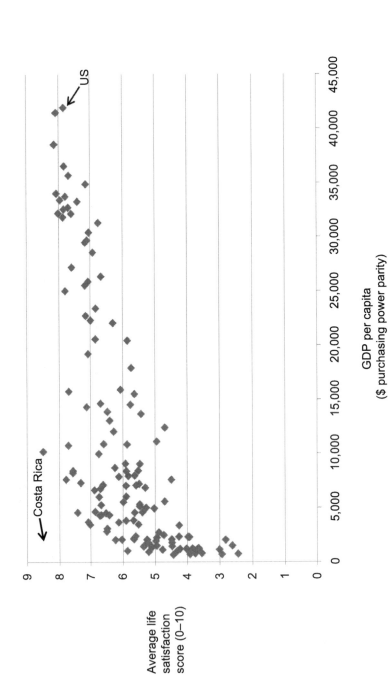

Figure 6.1 Relationship between life satisfaction and GDP per capita ($ purchasing power parity).
Sources: Data from FAO and the New Economics Foundation.

as "food secure" when its food comes at great expense to the ecological productive base that makes agriculture (and human welfare more generally) possible.

The FHSI includes two sustainability indicators. The one addressed in this section is that of total per capita water food-print as a percentage of total per capita renewable fresh water. The second indicator—daily per capita consumption of oils, fats, and sugars—will be elaborated upon shortly. The former ecological indicator looks at countries' total per capita water food-print as a percentage of their total per capita renewable freshwater supplies (see Table 6.1). It is calculated by taking a country's total virtual water food-print per capita and dividing it by its renewable freshwater resources per capita. A country's total virtual water food-print per capita is the sum total of its "green," "blue," and "grey" water food-prints for domestically and internationally sourced food (these water types are defined in Chapter 3).

Table 6.1 brings to light the remarkable variability between countries in terms of the sustainability of their respective water food-prints. For instance, Egypt's total per capita water food-print is 53.7 times greater than its total per capita renewable domestic fresh water (measured in cubic meters). In other words, Egyptians are consuming food, on a per capita basis, at a rate 53.7 times greater than what the country's freshwater stores could provide were all its food grown domestically. The United Arab Emirates—another grossly unsustainable water food-print—has a total per capita water food-print that is 49.5 times greater than what its domestic freshwater sources could sustain. Compare this to Iceland. Its total water per capita food-print is a mere 0.31 percent of its total per capita renewable freshwater reserves. Or take, for another example, the US. While it consumes more calories per capita than any other country, its total per capita water food-print as a percentage of total per capita renewable fresh water is roughly 28.8 percent. With this indicator, the US benefits considerably from the geophysical fact that it is water rich, especially relative to countries in the Middle East, which are water poor. The US case is a good example for why two ecological indicators are included in the FHSI. According to this water food-print indicator, the US is operating well within its ecological limits. But the unsustainability of the US food system is picked up, and the country is penalized accordingly, in the second ecological indicator, where daily per capita consumption of oils, fats, and sugars is factored into the equation.

In an attempt to standardize the data, the aforementioned water food-print percentages were ascribed a value. The rationale for this

Table 6.1 Total per capita fresh water food-print as a percent of total per capita renewable water (top twenty in bold) (m³)

Iceland	**0.310925**	Estonia	16.51885
Guyana	**0.463958**	Nepal	17.57755
Suriname	**0.737291**	Croatia	18.44257
Solomon Islands	**0.840152**	Slovenia	18.68922
Gabon	**1.255006**	Latvia	20.17891
Congo, Rep.	**1.375145**	Austria	20.28971
Norway	**1.492844**	Vietnam	20.65173
New Zealand	**1.803913**	Argentina	21.24511
Peru	**1.832024**	Tajikistan	22.88096
Chile	**2.055273**	Switzerland	23.79939
Canada	**2.235956**	Philippines	24.21844
Liberia	**2.27056**	Mozambique	25.39705
Nicaragua	**2.592148**	Korea, Dem. Rep.	26.14901
Colombia	**2.645574**	Mongolia	28.80105
Panama	**2.833502**	United States	28.81734
Belize	**3.328909**	Lithuania	29.23539
Cen. African Rep.	**3.635219**	Côte d'Ivoire	32.08335
Congo, Dem. Rep.	**3.908633**	El Salvador	32.69854
Costa Rica	**4.927414**	Japan	34.8435
Fiji	**5.123461**	Belarus	39.91698
Sierra Leone	5.128947	Thailand	40.42675
Russian Federation	5.560977	Greece	41.2503
Myanmar	5.713543	Macedonia, FYR	43.11556
Finland	5.808745	Cuba	44.89565
Ecuador	5.848269	Jamaica	45.78536
Venezuela	6.027668	Kazakhstan	46.07092
Sweden	6.687868	China	46.62717
Guinea	6.862971	UK	46.99359
Brazil	6.870289	Sri Lanka	47.76881
Cameroon	8.624576	Turkey	47.77913
Honduras	8.959642	Gambia, The	49.13131
Madagascar	9.161266	Mali	49.223
Australia	9.495994	Togo	49.79357
Malaysia	9.639907	Mexico	49.86648
Ireland	10.3169	France	50.07557
Guinea-Bissau	10.89139	Slovak Republic	50.66794
Bolivia	11.07427	Tanzania	52.25686
Angola	11.91668	Trinidad and Tobago	52.4241
Guatemala	12.20631	Armenia	53.09702
Cambodia	12.41807	Senegal	53.16254
Bosnia and Herzegovina	12.65526	Burundi	57.50254
		Dominican Republic	59.13716
Indonesia	12.78043	Namibia	59.37643
Paraguay	12.92753	Swaziland	60.22679
Uruguay	13.5924	Portugal	65.89199
Zambia	14.0694	Lesotho	66.61771
Georgia	15.09562	Italy	67.87557
Brunei Darussalam	15.29747	Bulgaria	72.467
Albania	15.87013	Romania	75.14416

Ethiopia	77.24832	The Netherlands	189.1231
Haiti	77.43776	Uzbekistan	190.5102
Comoros	78.40977	Cape Verde	201.1132
India	81.01259	Kenya	206.0383
Malawi	82.15477	Burkina Faso	216.345
Nigeria	85.739	Antigua and	233.4755
Poland	87.11717	Barbuda	
Rwanda	88.35623	Sudan	240.704
Uganda	88.80038	Cyprus	298.3301
Mauritius	90.00616	Hungary	364.6023
Ukraine	92.79638	Pakistan	400.113
Ghana	93.25655	Moldova	419.4376
Benin	93.72615	Algeria	479.5854
Spain	95.20944	Tunisia	539.1999
Germany	96.39995	Syrian Arab Republic	562.3369
Iran, Islamic Rep.	99.8952	Barbados	596.4603
Bangladesh	103.1803	Turkmenistan	792.6663
Chad	106.1975	Yemen, Rep.	980.3836
Luxembourg	109.394	Maldives	1348.921
Korea, Rep.	112.0642	Jordan	1380.964
Azerbaijan	113.8419	Niger	1501.354
Zimbabwe	116.409	Malta	1635.169
Czech Republic	118.3407	Saudi Arabia	1907.92
Belgium	127.3754	Libya	1985.424
South Africa	129.592	Mauritania	2104.172
Denmark	131.2958	Israel	2162.802
Botswana	163.9749	Bahamas	3089.918
Lebanon	172.806	United Arab Emirates	4949.472
Morocco	183.7063	Egypt, Arab Rep.	5372.204

Source: Hoekstra et al., 2011.

was twofold. First, if this were not done, countries such as Egypt would be unduly punished for their dependency on virtual water. It was also desirable to keep the values of each indicator close to a scale of 0 to 100; otherwise, there was the very real risk that one indicator would have disproportionate influence in the final calculation of the FHSI. Countries with a percentage greater than 500 were given a score of –25. (Egypt, for example, with a total water food-print 5,372 *percent* greater than its renewable freshwater food-print, received such a score.) These countries clearly need to be penalized, as it is inconceivable to label "food secure" any country that consumes water via food at a rate that is at least five times greater than what its domestic renewable freshwater sources would allow. Countries with a percentage between 201 and 500 were given a score of zero. Those with a percentage between 101 and 200 were given a score of 25. While possessing a total water food-print per capita greater than

what their own renewable freshwater capacity would allow, countries scoring 25 are at least close to consuming within their domestic
water budget. Those countries with a percentage between 76 and 100
were given a score of 50; between 51 and 75, a score of 75; and
between 26 and 50, a score of 100. Finally, those countries with a per
capita water food-print of 25 percent or less were given a score of
125 (not only to reward them but also to provide some symmetry to
this measure as the low-end extends to –25).

Potential for food independence

Trade dependency, for reasons elaborated upon in Chapter 5, is also
a variable worth including in discussions about genuine food security. The "Washington Consensus," as it has come to be known,
involves coercing less affluent nations into abandoning the practice
of surplus storage while gutting all government support programs
directed specifically at smallholders, such as those that provide subsidies for fertilizer and seed and the ever-important credit. If a country
suffered crop failures, it was believed, they could always import
whatever food they needed. The recent volatility in agricultural
commodity markets has proved the folly of that assumption.
Unfortunately, it was a lesson learned at the expense of the poor, as
evidenced in 2009 when the world's hungry exceeded one billion for
the first time in the history of humankind.

  Measuring food dependence, however, is difficult. There is considerable available data on agricultural trade calculated in terms of dollars
and volume. Yet, the commodities included in these figures refer not
only to foodstuffs but also to agricultural commodities for industrial
purposes and biofuels. Moreover, the units of "dollars" and "volume"
are problematic: as for the former, exchange value is not the same as
use value; while, in terms of the latter, "volume traded" rarely equals
"food volume" (raw material traded often has to be processed and/or
slaughtered before it can be consumed). It is also very difficult to
distinguish, when looking at import/export data, between a country
that is food independent and a country that is simply starving, as both
import very little food. As discussed in the previous chapter, the FAO
does calculate an "import dependency ratio" (IDR) of countries
(imports/(production + imports – exports) × 100). Yet this figure, too,
is problematic. For instance, how the units (e.g., imports, production,
and exports) are measured—volume or units of dollars—changes the
outcome of the ratio. We also know that imported agricultural

commodities are not always destined for domestic markets but may be re-exported to another country. This strategy is often used to work around trade sanctions and avoid certain trade barriers. (For example, Firm X sends grain to India meant ultimately for re-exportation to Iran, as the country that Firm X resides within has a trade embargo with the Iranian government.) Fortunately, the FHSI is already employing an indicator that can double as a proxy for measuring food dependency: total per capita water food-print as a percentage of total per capita renewable fresh water. What is particularly valuable about this calculation is that it focuses solely on *food consumed* rather than on more gross measures of, say, agrifood commodities imported. Clearly, a country like Egypt, whose total per capita water food-print is 53.7 times greater than its total per capita renewable domestic fresh water, is heavily dependent upon world markets for its food. This is not to suggest that countries at the other extreme—like Iceland, Norway, and New Zealand—are entirely food *independent*. But it does seem to imply that they have a greater potential for food independence than the Egypts and United Arab Emirates of the world.

Nutritional well-being

We still need to distinguish between those countries that are not consuming enough, those consuming too much, and those consuming within parameters that are recommended by public health professionals. This brings me to daily per capita consumption of oils, fats, and sugars. Complete international data sets are hard to come by when looking for indicators of under- and over-nutrition. There are, as noted earlier, a number of indicators available that point to the severe under-consumption of food, like data looking at the prevalence of underweight children under the age of five (used by the United Nations Development Program) and the statistic calculating the proportion of the population below minimal level of dietary energy consumption (used by the FAO). These metrics essentially break the world down into two categories: those nations that have absolutely nothing and those that have at least something—not a terribly useful distinction when trying to rank countries. Likewise, statistics are available that compare average BMI across countries. Yet, those data sets are woefully incomplete as not all countries compile such figures. I am also well aware of the criticisms leveled at BMI and of the limitations that come from placing too much emphasis on it as a proxy for individual health and well-being (see Guthman, 2011).

I prefer to include in the FHSI a complete data set that provides an indicator of both under- and over-consumption; one that not only highlights countries at both extremes but allows for distinctions to be made between countries that fall somewhere in the middle. World Health Organization (WHO) data on the daily average per capita consumption of oils, fats, and sugars make this possible. But this data, as I detailed in Chapter 4, is more than just a proxy for nutritional well-being. It has also been conclusively established that bad diets—namely, those that are highly processed and exceed recommended daily allowances in (especially animal) fats—are bad for the environment. This metric also, therefore, doubles as a proxy measure of sustainability.

In order to incorporate this data set into the FHSI, however, it had to be standardized. This demanded a couple of assumptions. First, it was necessary to establish what could be considered an "optimal" average daily caloric intake. Individual differences in metabolic mechanisms and levels of activity (e.g., sedentary versus active/manual labor) make this exceedingly difficult and inherently problematic. On average, infants and children (below ten years of age) require fewer calories than adults; and females require fewer calories than males. And, as adults age, their caloric requirements gradually decrease. After carefully considering all the various metabolic demands (see Table 6.2),

Table 6.2 USDA caloric intake guidelines

| | Activity level | | | |
	Age (years)	Sedentary	Moderately active	Active
Child	2–3	1,000	1,000–1,400	1,000–1,400
Female	4–8	1,200	1,400–1,600	1,400–1,800
	9–13	1,600	1,600–2,000	1,800–2,200
	14–18	1,800	2,000	2,400
	19–30	2,000	2,000–2,200	2,400
	31–50	1,800	2,000	2,200
	51+	1,600	1,800	2,000–2,200
Male	4–8	1,400	1,400–1,600	1,600–2,000
	9–13	1,800	1,800–2,200	2,000–2,600
	14–18	2,200	2,400–2,800	2,800–3,200
	19–30	2,400	2,600–2,800	3,000
	31–50	2,200	2,400–2,600	2,800–3,000
	51+	2,000	2,200–2,400	2,400–2,800

Source: Adapted from USDA, 2005.

it seemed reasonable to settle upon 2,500 as an optimal daily per capita caloric intake.

Second, an optimal daily per capita caloric range for oils, fats, and sugars had to be calculated. The WHO recommends that no less than 15 percent and no more than 30 percent of one's daily caloric intake come from fats. Based on a diet of 2,500 kcal a day, that equates to no fewer than 375 kcal and no more than 750 kcal from fat. The WHO further recommends that no more than 8 percent of one's daily energy intake should be derived from sugar. In other words, based on a daily diet of 2,500 kcal, no more than 200 kcal should come from sugars. Combining these figures, we are left with an optimal oils, fats, and sugars daily caloric range of between 575 (375 + 200) and 950 (750 + 200).

Figure 6.2 examines the relationship between daily per capita consumption for oils, fats, and sugars and average life satisfaction. While the relationship between these two variables is fairly significant until 575 kcal (correlation coefficient of 0.51), it flattens out considerably between 575 and 950 kcal (correlation coefficient of 0.19), and turns negative after 950 kcal (correlation coefficient of −0.112).

A method then had to be devised to compare countries that do not fall within the optimal range, at both the high and low ends. Calculating the low end was straightforward, as 0 kcal from oils, fats, and sugars is an obvious base. But what top-end caloric figure would be comparable to a figure of zero? It could be argued that 2,000 kcal per day from oils, fats, and sugars is a suitable top-end total. Admittedly, it is ultimately a normative judgement to make an assessment of whether individual and societal welfare is comparable between societies that consume zero and 2,000 kcal daily from oils, fats, and sugars. The last step involved standardizing the data on a 100-point scale. Those countries that fell within the optimal range of between 575 and 950 kcal received a score of 100. Among those that fell below, a calculation was made based upon their location between the low end of the optimal range (575 kcal) and the base (0 kcal). Thus, for instance, if a country had a daily per capita caloric oil, fat, and sugar intake of 287.5 kcal, it received a 50 percent; whereas if the figure was, say, 517.5 kcal, it received a 90 percent (the closer to the optimal range the higher/better the score). For countries above the optimal range, the calculation was made in relation to their location between the high end of the optimal range (950 kcal) and the top (2,000 kcal). Thus, for instance, if a country had a daily per capita caloric oil, fat, and sugar intake of 1,475, it received a 50 percent (the

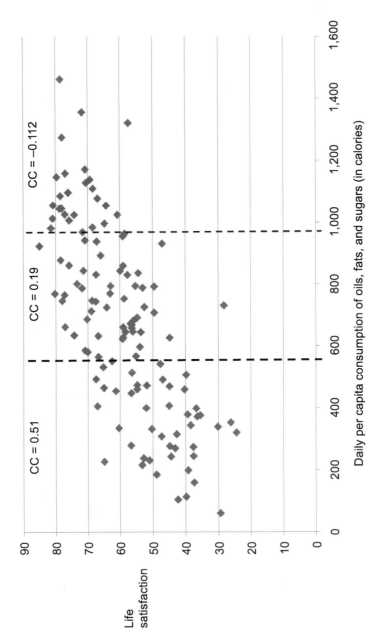

Figure 6.2 Relationship between daily per capita consumption of oils, fats, and sugars and life satisfaction

Note: CC = correlation coefficient.

Sources: Data from the WHO and the New Economics Foundation.

caloric intake for the US was 1,462, giving it a percentage of 51.3);
whereas if the caloric figure was 1,055, it received a 90 percent
(again, the closer to the optimal range the higher/better the score).

Freedom in agrifood chain

The last index serves as a proxy for food-system concentration:
supermarket concentration. More specific still, this index looks at the
CR5 ratio (or five-firm concentration ratio) for the retail food sector.
As discussed in Chapter 5, the CR5 reflects the sum of market shares
of the top five firms for a given industry. Wherever there is market
concentration there is an increased risk of market distortion in the
form of buyer and/or seller power, both of which can have deleterious effects on food access and food security more generally (see
Burch and Lawrence, 2007; Stringer and Le Heron, 2008).

As described in the previous chapter, the market power of large
retailers has become particularly pronounced in recent years. Given
the volume of their sales, large retail firms such as Walmart and Kroger
are dealing increasingly with a handful of very large packers, allowing
them to bypass the wholesale sector entirely. This not only cuts the
"middleman" out of the equation but allows retail firms to exploit the
buyer power held by the largest processing firms, who then pass the
tighter margins on to producers. This helps explain the growing gap
between what producers are paid and retail prices for those products.
A study from 2004 calculated that the difference between the price
paid to farmers and that paid by consumers increased by 149 percent
between 1970 and 1998 (Marsh and Brester, 2004). Retail concentration can also negatively affect individuals at the other end of the
agrifood chain: namely, consumers. Supermarket concentration,
particularly at the city or regional levels, has been linked to food
deserts (Blanchard and Matthews, 2008), higher food prices (Richards
and Pofahl, 2010), and reduced food choice (Hawkes, 2008).

Once food retail data were obtained and ratios calculated it was
necessary to establish what percentage of food sales are accounted
for by supermarkets in each country. A number of countries in South
America (Chile, for example) have significant levels of supermarket
concentration (CR5 ratios of over 50). Yet if, say, only 50 percent of
all food sales occur in a supermarket/retail context, it would be somewhat misleading to treat that nation as identical to one where the
figure is closer to 100 percent. CR5 ratios thus needed to be adjusted
(standardized) in some instances to take into account these

discrepancies. The goal was to arrive at a statistic that reflected a ratio of market concentration for each nation's *total* food sales (not just its supermarket/retail sales). The "mirror" CR5 statistic was then included in the FHSI to ensure this metric was in line with previous indicators, where higher numbers are desirable (thus, for example, Australia and New Zealand each had a supermarket concentration score of 1 in the FHSI).

Results

FHSI scores were arrived at by adding the five aforementioned variables and calculating their average. The results of this tabulation are contained in Table 6.3. Topping the list is Costa Rica. It has a higher life expectancy than that found in the US (78.5 versus 77.9) and the highest reported life satisfaction score of any country (85 out of 100). Its total water per capita food-print is a mere 4.9 percent of its total per capita renewable freshwater reserves. The daily per capita consumption of oils, fats, and sugars in Costa Rica is at the high end of the optimal range—923 kcal—and its food retail sector has a relatively low level of supermarket concentration at CR5 = 20.

Table 6.3 Final FHSI ranking (top twenty in bold)

Costa Rica	**77.69941**	Bosnia and Herzegovina	71.70576
Iceland	**76.9785**		
Finland	**76.82639**	Lithuania	71.02415
Ireland	**76.38799**	Peru	70.93786
Norway	**75.96306**	Uruguay	70.82868
Panama	**75.60614**	Ecuador	70.8148
Australia	**75.23405**	Mexico	70.55152
New Zealand	**74.78275**	Estonia	70.51097
Slovenia	**74.48956**	Austria	70.318
Sweden	**74.24623**	Indonesia	70.27923
Argentina	**74.23092**	Latvia	70.26255
Colombia	**74.12041**	Japan	69.9647
Guatemala	**73.8**	Russia	69.73279
Nicaragua	**73.56197**	Guyana	69.7025
Brazil	**73.4256**	United Kingdom	69.23483
Canada	**73.27342**	Jamaica	67.88
Chile	**73.23772**	Albania	67.66962
Paraguay	**72.99126**	El Salvador	67.62095
Malaysia	**72.93622**	Bolivia	67.12047
Honduras	**72.92498**	France	66.77313
Croatia	72.8803	Greece	66.43562
Switzerland	72.68762	Philippines	66.18093

Thailand	65.58672	Cyprus	49.7586
Slovakia	65.58326	Madagascar	49.677
Belarus	65.40359	Togo	49.08168
Turkey	65.32289	Congo, Dem. Rep.	48.92
Sri Lanka	65.09939	Lebanon	48.71698
Dominican Republic	64.45163	Haiti	48.712
Cuba	64.02	Namibia	48.476
Venezuela	63.419	Bangladesh	48.12083
China	62.02574	Nigeria	47.70454
Portugal	62.00208	Mali	47.67466
Guinea	61.554	Chad	45.79439
United States of America	61.54381	Algeria	45.51621
Italy	61.34197	South Africa	45.06294
Kazakhstan	61.26534	United Arab	45.02
Romania	61.22323	Emirates	
Vietnam	60.619	Malta	44.98807
Bulgaria	60.4792	Pakistan	44.12322
Trinidad and Tobago	59.82946	Egypt	42.14337
Spain	58.5241	Uzbekistan	42.08304
Central African Republic	57.8	Ghana	42.00219
Poland	57.13814	Tunisia	41.48529
Tajikistan	56.50004	Syria	41.44615
Senegal	56.42497	Jordan	41.35508
Cameroon	56.01828	Tanzania	41.22243
Nepal	55.67337	Botswana	41.13291
Saudi Arabia	54.82	Israel	41.01647
The Netherlands	54.83722	Hungary	40.7091
Denmark	54.73759	Moldova	40.56666
Mongolia	54.20514	Benin	38.90501
Ukraine	54.14168	Zimbabwe	38.83415
Sierra Leone	53.54083	Uganda	38.53404
India	53.48482	Mauritania	37.54381
Czech Republic	53.24123	Azerbaijan	37.25394
Mozambique	53.20794	Sudan	36.806
Korea	53.19107	Malawi	36.592
Iran	53.18516	Burundi	32.66943
Angola	52.82819	Ethiopia	32.24761
Cambodia	52.81402	Kenya	31.64347
Germany	52.45637	Yemen	31.612
Zambia	51.11917	Rwanda	31.11954
Armenia	50.94918	Burkina Faso	30.49701
Morocco	50.3491	Niger	22.18942

Between the FHSI and the preceding chapters there is, I realize, a lot to unpack and make sense of as we reimagine food security for the twenty-first century. In the preceding chapters, I labored to empirically upend what has long been viewed as "common sense" in many agrifood circles, showing the problematic relationships between such issues as productivism, trade, and growth and food security and human welfare. Now, in this chapter, I have presented a food security index that places a country like the US in the middle of the pack (below such countries as China, Cuba, and Jamaica), while Costa Rica, Iceland, and Finland rank first, second, and third, respectively. What is going on here?

In the final chapter, I attempt to answer this question while inviting further debate. I do this by beginning the process of fleshing out what genuine food security ought to mean, so that we might use this reclaimed understanding to enhance the resilience of food futures around the world. It is not my intention to suggest that the world ought to emulate Costa Rica as far as domestic agrifood policies go. But equally, based upon everything we have seen up to this point, we have to question certain core convictions concerning whom we have long viewed as worthy of emulation. Over the last fifty-plus years, we have held steadfast to a belief about what food security constitutes. Based upon everything that has been covered thus far in this book, we can say quite definitively that our loyalty to this belief has been misplaced. It is time for a change.

Chapter 7

Lessons learned

In 1980, ex-Chancellor of Germany, Willy Brandt, chaired a commission that produced a report entitled *North–South: A Programme for Survival*. The report presents a world with a clear dividing line between the rich, influential North and the poor, marginalized South in need of continual international assistance. While the world is drastically different today when compared to 1980, the image of the Global South, as it is called, remains much the same (Williams et al., 2009). This is especially the case when talking about food security. Take the UN-sponsored book *Food Security*, in which the authors offhandedly remark (as if the claim does not even require empirical justification) that "the extent of hunger and food insecurity [in the US] is much less severe than in the developing world" (Dutta and Gundersen, 2007, p. 44). Fortunately, not everyone has fallen into this North/South trap. Scholars of agroecology (e.g., Altieri, 2004) and international peasant movements like La Via Campesina (e.g., McMichael, 2006) have provided convincing documentation that a country's location in the so-called Global South does not automatically place it in the category of "food insecure." Elsewhere, it is being argued with increasing intensity that high-income nations should not be assumed to be food secure merely because they are awash in cheap, fatty, sugary calories (e.g., Carolan, 2011b). The previous chapters—including Chapter 6—lend considerable empirical support to the view that conventional wisdom is often wrong when it comes to delineating between those countries that are food secure and those that are not.

I want to end this book by building on what was started in Chapter 6 with the FHSI. Specifically, the aim of this chapter is to investigate further what genuine food security looks like, based upon what we have learned up to this point. I build this narrative from the ground up, starting within the farm gate but eventually working well beyond it. I have already addressed the limits of the green revolution in earlier chapters. In the next section, I review alternatives to it, arguing that we need a rainbow evolution instead. Yet, as I have argued repeatedly, food security—*real* food security—cannot be achieved by merely tweaking production methods. The vast majority of this chapter is therefore devoted to covering subjects that have nothing to do with either farming or agriculture more generally.

Remember, we are talking about *food* security, which means we are talking about something that essentially impacts every facet of social life. Discussion therefore quickly moves beyond the farm gate—and beyond even the food system—by providing a response to the admittedly thorny question: so what can we eat if not GDP? This question is based on a wealth of empirical evidence (presented earlier) that shows the uneasy relationship between economic growth and food security.

The third section builds upon this discussion by pushing for a thoroughly sociological rendering of food security. I argue that it ought not to be viewed as a thing—or an end in itself—but as a process that makes people and the planet better off. Once we start understanding "food security" as a verb—rather than a noun—we can begin to assess the respective food-scapes of nations honestly. And, in the end, image food futures that reclaim the original spirit of food security.

From green revolution to rainbow evolutions

In 2002, then UN Secretary General Kofi Annan asked an appointed panel of experts from such countries as Brazil, China, Mexico, and South Africa how a green revolution could be achieved in Africa. After more than a year of study, the group had their answer. Foremost, they questioned the one-size-fits-all approach to food security taken by the green revolution: "The diverse African situation implies that no single magic 'technological bullet' is available for radically improving African agriculture" (InterAcademy Council, 2003, p. xviii). The panel's strategic recommendations explain that "African agriculture is more likely to experience numerous rainbow evolutions that differ in nature and extent among the many systems, rather than one Green Revolution as in Asia" (InterAcademy Council, 2003, p. xviii).

While Annan went on to reject the panel's recommendation—by agreeing shortly thereafter to head the Alliance for a Green Revolution in Africa funded by the Bill and Melinda Gates Foundation—this is the direction we ought to be heading. If the green revolution taught us anything, it was that magic bullets exist only in the movies. And as for calls for a *greener* revolution (which hinges heavily upon biotechnology), if the green revolution effectively made food security worse in some parts of the world—as detailed in Chapter 2—then why would not more of the same? This is not to say that biotechnology cannot play a role. It just should not be given the sole role in food security initiatives—after all, the many barriers to food security cannot merely be bred (or genetically engineered) away (see Box 7.1).

To explain my unease toward the green revolution in even simpler terms (by repeating a point made earlier): we need more alternatives, not fewer. There is too much at stake to gamble on a bet that effectively reduces our options. Genuine food security lies in more choice, not less, which is why the term "rainbow evolutions" is so apt. Why go just "green" when we could go "rainbow"? The word "rainbow" draws attention away from the magic-bullet solution, while "evolutions" (note the plural) emphasizes local conditions, as opposed to the overthrow of those conditions (as "revolution" implies). Context is everything. And those systems designed to adapt to (rather than change) it will always end up more robust and resilient in the long run.

Box 7.1 Food security and the AIDS epidemic

The AIDS/HIV epidemic is having a significant impact on food security in Africa by undermining rural household income production (for the ill as well as for their care-givers), lowering agricultural output, and negatively affecting the integrity of families and their sustainability as viable units (Baylies, 2002; Fox et al., 2004). The disease also changes household spending and investment decisions. Sick households tend to reduce agricultural investment to pay for healthcare (Donovan et al., 2003), which helps explain the link that has been made between the southern African famine of the 1990s and the region's AIDS epidemic (Negin et al., 2009). Gender and nutrition play central roles in these outcomes. African women are disproportionately impacted by the epidemic as well as by the aforementioned changes to household spending and agricultural decision-making. At the same time, the AIDS/HIV epidemic has increased their responsibilities in terms of agricultural and care labor as individuals living with the disease have greater nutrition needs (Negin et al., 2009). Food preparation in these instances becomes as important as food cultivation. While not often thought of in these terms, some phenomenal gains in food security for African countries ravaged by AIDS/HIV could be achieved by placing their infected individuals on treatment regimes. Such a practice has been shown more than to double the number of days per month that AIDS/HIV-positive farmers work (Larson et al., 2008). Another obvious issue on which to focus would be to help women secure land ownership and access to credit and markets in the event of the death of the male head of household (Negin et al., 2009).

For an example of how context matters, take livestock agriculture. While Chapter 4 is rather critical of this sector, we have to realize that it is not livestock agriculture *per se* that is problematic. What *is* problematic is how we currently go about producing animal protein throughout much of the world with very little regard of total through-puts. At its worse, the industrial beef cow consumes as much as 100,000 liters of water per kilogram of live weight gained (Pimentel et al., 1997). Then you have the opposite extreme: extensive (versus intensive) beef production in northern Africa. The average cow in a typical northern African system consumes 25 liters of water per day over a two-year period to produce 125 kg of meat, while living off crop residues (for which no additional water input is required). This equates to a direct water consumption of 146 liters per kilogram. Under the most extreme hot/dry conditions, direct consumption could double to slightly less than 300 liters per kilogram. Yet even these figures overstate matters, as much of the water consumed by these animals is recycled back into the soil as urine, providing important soil nutrients as well as moisture (Rosegrant et al., 2005).

Table 7.1 details population and land use by region. Note the variability in food-supporting land types. Some regions are well endowed with arable land, such as Europe, Russia, and North America. Other areas are arable-land poor but rich in permanent pasture. In sub-Saharan Africa, for example, only 17 percent of land is arable, with most of the remainder in permanent pasture. For this region in particular, livestock agriculture may well play a central role in food security as animals are to a certain degree the only food that may be

Table 7.1 Population and land use by region (2006)

Region	Population	Agricultural land (ha)	% Arable	% Permanent pasture
Sub-Saharan Africa	750,500,000	947,000,000	17.0	80.8
China and India	2,480,300,000	736,000,000	41.2	55.9
Asia (other)	1,503,000,000	635,000,000	24.8	68.7
Australia/ New Zealand	24,700,000	457,000,000	10.8	88.7
Europe	588,100,000	267,000,000	60.4	34.0
Russia	143,200,000	216,000,000	56.7	42.5
Latin America/ Caribbean	565,000,000	726,000,000	19.7	77.6
North Africa	408,800,000	458,000,000	19.1	78.4
North America	335,500,000	477,000,000	45.9	52.3
World	6,592,800,000	4,973,000,000	28.2	69.0

Source: Data from Peterson, 2009, p. 54.

"grown" there. Notice also the lack of arable agricultural land in the tropics. Tropical soils are generally of a poorer quality than temperate-zone soils, where most of the biological diversity is actually contained in the soil, making it remarkably fertile. In the tropics, conversely, much of the life is above ground, making for soil that becomes easily depleted and slow to rejuvenate (Achard et al., 2002). The green revolution, however, was blind to this context, wishing instead to blanket the world in high-yielding cereals regardless of local agroecological conditions.

We also know that small-scale, diverse farmers fare quite well when compared to conventional agricultural systems; in fact, in terms of harvestable products per unit area, they often outproduce large, specialized operations by between 20 and 60 percent (Altieri and Nicholls, 2008). Gliessman (1998) notes that a 1.73-ha plot of land in Mexico planted in corn produces as much food as a 1-ha plot planted with a mixture of corn, squash, and beans. In Brazil, fields planted with both corn (at 12,500 plants per hectare) and soybeans (at 150,000 plants per hectare) exhibited a 28 percent yield advantage over a comparable soybean monoculture (Altieri, 1999). This inverse relationship between farm size and productivity has been attributed to a more efficient use of land, water, biodiversity (e.g., keeping intact internal ecological pest controls, thus eliminating the need for pesticides), and other agricultural resources by small farmers.

Small, diverse farms are also less vulnerable to catastrophic loss due to environmental events—an attribute of considerable importance in light of the growing threat of climate-change-related weather events (Alexander, 2008).

Agroecological principles also lie at the center of many organic farms, which explains, when managed properly, their favorable comparison to conventional methods of food production. Badgley and colleagues (2007) examined approximately three hundred studies from around the world comparing organic and conventional farming systems and their respective yields. Based upon this extensive review, they concluded that organic agriculture has the potential to feed the world, noting that organic systems can produce yields comparable to (or in some cases even better than) conventional operations. Granted, these smaller, more diverse farms are more labor-intensive than their energy-intensive competitors. But we have to remember that their own labor is often one of the few things (sometimes the only thing) that peasant farmers possess. What they tend to lack is access to the capital and credit necessary to follow in the unsustainable food-prints of the green revolution.

Our bias toward the status quo runs so deep that it even infiltrates how we frame our questions about food and potential food futures. Take the various economic studies conducted over the years to assess the benefits of pesticides. The seemingly objective goal set out to be attained in these studies typically involves assessing the economic impacts were pesticides to be banned outright (see, e.g., Settle, 1983; Cooper and Dobson, 2007). Not surprisingly, if pesticides were banned today, farm output would suffer. But think about *why* this would be the case. The conventional system has become dependent upon these external controls because of agroecological realities of its own making, leading to what has been called the "pesticide tread-mill" (Van den Bosch, 1978). This speaks to the well-documented phenomenon of how insects evolve to become resistant to pesticides. This in turn leads to more applications and/or higher concentrations and/or new chemicals, which in turn lead to still further resistance, and so on. Pesticides have created a vicious cycle that will perpetually be fought out (literally) between pest ecology and pesticide companies, with each "side" continually evolving in response to the other.

Therefore, any ban on pesticides must be accompanied with broader changes to *the system*. Only then will pesticides no longer be needed, as the aforementioned treadmill will have been dismantled. Besides, it is wholly unrealistic to assume a total and immediate ban on pesticides would ever take place. The far more likely scenario would involve a transition period, where new technologies replace old and where internal controls are given time to build up again. Researchers who choose to phrase the pesticide question in terms of an outright ban therefore might as well be asking about the grain–protein conversion ratio of unicorns in CAFOs, as the two scenarios are equally mythical in character.

So what can we eat if not GDP?

A significant body of peer-reviewed literature has emerged in the last few years that sticks a pin in the balloon of orthodoxy. Beyond offering a critique of economic growth—which is not new—this research provides conclusive evidence that affluence beyond a certain level becomes at best unconnected to individual and societal well-being indicators and at worst may even be *negatively* associated with human welfare (see Jackson, 2009; Knight and Rosa, 2011; Dietz et al., 2012). Economist Herman Daly (1999) calls this "uneconomic growth": growth that costs us more than the benefits we accrue from it. The data presented in earlier chapters support this argument, as does the FHSI.

Figure 7.1 plots the relationship between FHSI and GDP per capita. Taking all 126 countries collectively reveals a moderate positive relationship between FHSI and GDP per capita (a correlation coefficient of 0.359). Yet something very interesting reveals itself when we examine countries going from lowest GDP per capita to highest. Among countries with a GDP per capita of US$10,000 or greater, the relationship largely flattens out (a correlation coefficient of 0.164). Then, among countries with a GDP per capita of US$30,000 or greater, the relationship is non-existent (a correlation coefficient of 0.078).

This leads to the all-important question: what *can* be eaten if not GDP per capita? A growing body of research points to how inequality negatively affects a society's ability to improve the welfare of its citizenry efficiently. For example, more equal societies, to take a couple of examples from Wilkinson and Pickett's (2009) acclaimed *The Spirit Level*, have fewer health and social problems, treat children better, treat women more equally, have a greater sense of collective responsibility, have lower levels of mental illness, and are more likely to produce business leaders who agree that their governments should cooperate with international environmental agreements (an

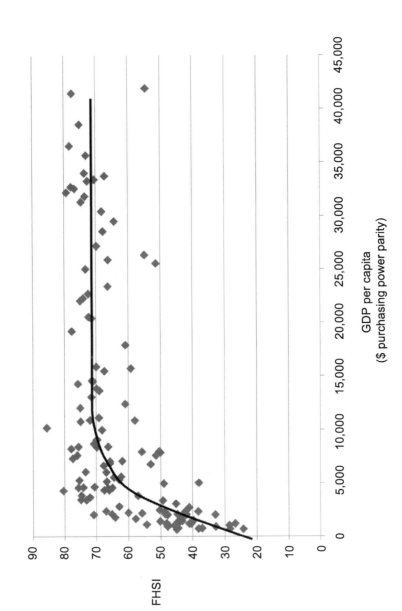

Figure 7.1 Relationship between FHSI and GDP per capita ($ purchasing power parity).

Source: Data from FAO.

important quality in an age of anthropogenic climate change) (see also Wilkinson et al., 2010).

Inspired by this research, FHSI scores were plotted against national levels of inequality as measured by the gini coefficient—a numerical measure of income inequality ranging from 0 (absolute equality) to 1 (absolute inequality). When all 126 countries were viewed collectively, a very weak negative relationship was found between the variables (correlation coefficient of –0.071). As lower-income countries were removed, however, the strength of that negative relationship grew significantly. Among countries with a GDP per capita of US$20,000 or greater, the correlation coefficient was –0.285. Among countries with a GDP per capita of US$25,000 or greater, it was –0.426. Finally, among the highest-income countries—namely, those with a GDP per capita of US$35,000 or greater—the correlation coefficient was a stunningly robust –0.97.

Inequality therefore appears to have a remarkably corrosive effect on a country's ability to ensure its population is (and feels) food secure (see Box 7.2). So why is that the case? Fortunately, we can look to the literature for an explanation. We know, for example, that more equal societies are, among other things, happier and have higher life expectancies than less equal societies (Wilkinson and Pickett, 2009). There is also considerable evidence that inequality is detrimental to dietary health, fruit and vegetable consumption, and the consumption of nutritiously dense foods more generally (Rose and Richards, 2004; Drewnowski and Darmon, 2005b; Morton et al., 2005). Thanks to decades of food policy fetishization of the calorie, agrifood chains around the world have evolved to a point where many countries (especially affluent ones) have an inverse relationship between energy density (kcal/kg) and energy cost ($/kcal) (Carolan, 2011b). In other words, energy-dense (nutrient-shallow) foods represent the lowest-cost option for many consumers. This provides an explanation for why the highest rates of obesity in affluent counties occur among population groups with the highest poverty rates and the least education (Drewnowski and Specter, 2004). Public health professionals tell us we should eat less of certain foods, but it turns out that these are the only foods the poor can afford in significant quantities. If low-income households in the US wanted to meet fruit and vegetable consumption government guidelines close to three-fourths of their total food budget would have to be spent on these items (Cassady et al., 2007). And they would still have three food groups to go.

Box 7.2 Income inequality and food security

We have done a great disservice to billions of people by focusing so intently on food security as a problem of supply. The theory goes that if we just produce more, which will therefore make food cheaper, then everything else will take care of itself. But if by making more cheap food we are depressing incomes around the world, are we really gaining any ground? While rarely noted in debates today around either subject, income inequality looks to contribute to food insecurity by way of multiple causal pathways (see, e.g., Alkon and Agyeman, 2011; Gottlieb, 2010).

While most people believe extreme poverty to be morally wrong, the morality of inequality is far from settled terrain. While differential reward—especially when that reward is equally available to all—encourages people to make the world a better place, research (and common sense) indicates that too much inequality stifles innovation. Getting the level of differential reward "right" is therefore not only an ethical question but one with profound practical consequences (Gilding, 2011). To help us think through this question, Herman Daly (1996) offers the following instructive observation. He proposes a factor of ten as an inequality ceiling. The military and universities have managed to keep their ratios close to or even below this level while maintaining tremendous drive among their individual members. In the US military, for instance, the highest-paid generals make roughly ten times the wages of a private. In a university, the prized rank of distinguished professor brings with it a salary that is roughly six to eight times that of a full-time non-tenure-track instructor. Compare this to the corporate world, and specifically Walmart: in 2007 its CEO (H. Lee Scott) made US$29,682,000—that's 1,314 times more than the company's average full-time workers (IPS, 2008). It is also roughly 150 times more than a top-ranking US general or a distinguished professor. Is the CEO of Walmart 150 times more motivated than a US general or a distinguished professor? Do we believe he (H. Lee Scott) delivers 150 times more value to society than a top military commander or, say, a Nobel Prize-winning professor?

Gender inequality is also of serious consequence to the food security of women and girls the world over. A study of the eating habits of more than two thousand teenagers aged between thirteen and seventeen in the south of Ethiopia revealed that the girls suffered more than boys from general weakness and pathologies due to gender-based insecurity (Sasson, 2012). Pietr Van Dooren, of the Institute of Tropical Medicine in Antwerp, Belgium, is quoted as stating, "in an Ethiopian family, the boy is often perceived as having a more important economic and religious role to play; people tend to believe that he will be more productive and more able to manage the household in case of crisis" (Sasson, 2012, p. 5). A nutritionist working for UNICEF in West Africa gives a similarly bleak assessment of the food-scape faced by women in rural Ethiopia: "In a context of food insecurity, the social status of women raises many problems. Men [it is believed] should receive the best food, while women eat leftovers, and generally food of lesser quality" (Sasson, 2012, p. 5).

Women workers are also more dependent than male workers on agriculture for survival. Among women in least developed countries who are economically active, roughly 80 percent report agriculture as their primary economic activity. Among all economically active women in the world, 48 percent report that their primary activity is agriculture (Doss, 2011). In Africa, 63 percent of female workers depend on agriculture-based livelihoods, compared to 48 percent of male workers. In Asia, the figures are 57 percent and 48 percent, respectively. In India, 83 percent of rural female workers are employed in agriculture (Agarwal, 2011). And as the structure of agriculture has changed it has become *even more feminized* throughout much of the world. As food policy has sought to eliminate peasant agriculture those who remain tend to be the individuals with the fewest opportunities for education, credit, and skilled jobs—an agrarian transition that has been highly gendered. Except for in Europe, the past four decades have seen women workers rising as a proportion of the total agricultural workforce (Agarwal, 2011). But even this understates the role women play in national food systems. Time-use data for parts of sub-Saharan Africa, India, and China show that if we include time spent on food production, processing, and preparation, women contribute 60 to 70 percent of the total labor needed to bring food to the table (Doss, 2011).

Promoting policies that actively seek to push individuals out of agriculture—what has been referred to as freeing individuals from "shackles" (e.g., Ellis, 2005, p. 144)—inflicts irreparable harm on those populations who are dependent upon agriculture for their livelihood and for whom alternatives are scarce, such as women. And yet, while tied to agriculture (and food production/preparation more generally), women lack access to certain basic necessities that further complicates their freedom to pursue activities to enhance their well-being. Take the issue of land ownership. Throughout much of South Asia—save for Sri Lanka—few women own land (Agarwal, 1994). Yet ownership is just part of the battle; owning something and having control over it, particularly when that something is land and the owner is a woman, are frequently two separate issues. Related to this are the well-documented gendered inequalities relating to access to technical information, credit, extension services, inputs such as fertilizers and water, and market outlets (World Bank, 2009). Women owning land have also been found to be at significantly lower risk of facing domestic violence, which in turn has been found to improve the food security of the women and children in those households as such violence tends to have a negative effect on the nutritional health of the victims (Agarwal and Panda, 2007). In sum, a considerable body of evidence supports the pro-food security consequences that would accompany the reduction of gender inequalities, particularly those pertaining to access to land (and land rights more generally), support systems, credit, and markets (Agarwal, 2010).

Care also has to be taken not to be lulled into the belief that affluent nations, simply by nature of their affluence, ought to be emulated when it comes to issues of gender equality. For the evidence indicates that food insecurity is also feminized in fully developed nations. Figure 7.2 plots the relationship between the gender inequality index (GII) and GDP per capita among the world's most affluent nations. The GII, for those unfamiliar with this measure, reflects women's disadvantage in the areas of reproductive health, empowerment, and the labor market. It ranges from 0, which indicates that women and men fare equally, to 1, which indicates that women fare as poorly as possible in all measured dimensions. After US$35,000 GDP per capita, national-level affluence is *positively* correlated with gender inequality (its correlation coefficient is 0.353). Women, in other words, are more likely to be *worse off* the more affluent a country becomes after US$35,000 GDP per capita.

Finally, Figure 7.3 examines the relationship between gender inequality and the FHSI for those countries with a GII score. It should come as no surprise, in light of all that has been mentioned, that FHSI and GII scores are moderately negatively correlated (with a correlation coefficient of −0.443).

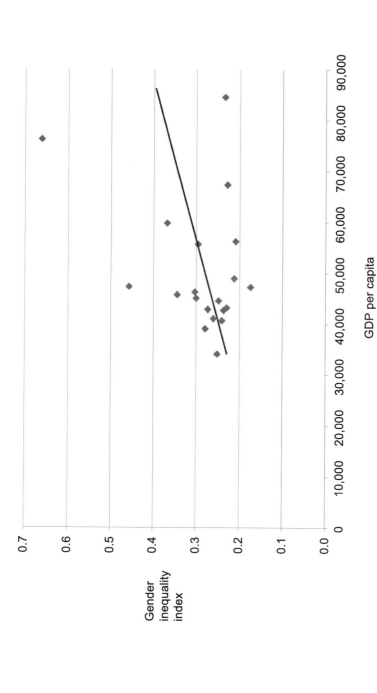

Figure 7.2 Relationship between gender inequality index and GDP per capita (US$35,000 and greater).

Sources: Data from FAO and Central Intelligence Agency.

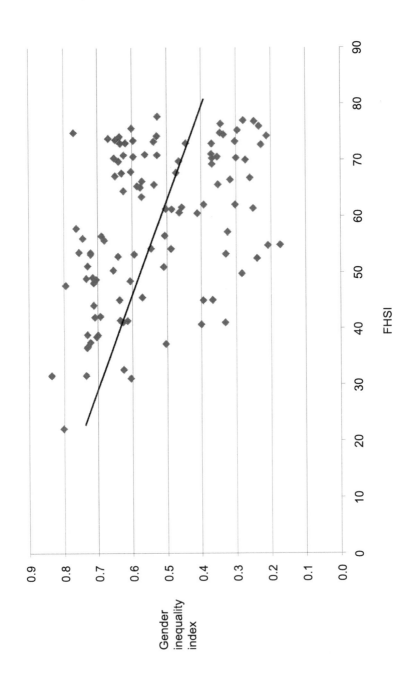

Figure 7.3 Relationship between gender inequality index and FHSI.
Source: Data from FAO.

Food security as a process (not a thing)

One of my goals has been to force open the concept of food security in the hope of reclaiming it from the clutches of neoliberalism, the productivist ideology, and caloric reductionism. Chapters 3 through 5 showed that many of the promises of conventional agrifood policy ring hollow. Then, in Chapter 6, I introduced the FHSI. Without claiming to measure the admittedly nebulous concept exhaustively, one of the strengths of the FHSI is that it embraces many of the concerns that at present cause countless scholars and practitioners to be critical of "food security," as it is currently understood. At the very least, the FHSI provides a conceptual reminder of the limits of current conventional thinking about the concept.

Regardless of whether you think Costa Rica is more food secure than, say, Canada, Mexico, New Zealand, Sweden, or the US, the FHSI is based on *objective* indicators that cannot be summarily dismissed out of hand. Based on these indicators, Costa Rica has accomplished something quite impressive, as have many other countries with high FHSI scores. Gleaning lessons from those countries with high FHSI scores, as well as perhaps some suggestions on what to avoid (especially among countries with low FHSI scores and high GDP per capita), could prove fruitful as the issue of food security continues to grow in both salience and importance.

Figures 7.4 and 7.5 provide spider charts of FHSI indices for the US and Costa Rica, respectively. The fuller the chart, the higher are the respective scores for the five indices described in the previous chapter (terms in bold reflect what the data are proxies for). Looking "within" FHSI scores and presenting the data in this manner provides another way of comparing food-scapes across countries, which could be used to direct policy better. As the figures illustrate, while Costa Rica scores high across all five categories, the results for the US are more mixed. According to the US spider chart, targeting agrifood concentration and the types of foods produced and consumed would go a long way toward improving the food and human security situation in that country.

We have also learned in the previous chapters that food security is not about being in possession of any particular *things*. Food security is not like a cake—you cannot just write the ingredients down for the world to follow. In fact, as I began to argue earlier in this chapter, food security is about more than just food. The data presented in the previous chapters (including the FHSI), while attempting to open up

Figure 7.4 US FHSI indices.

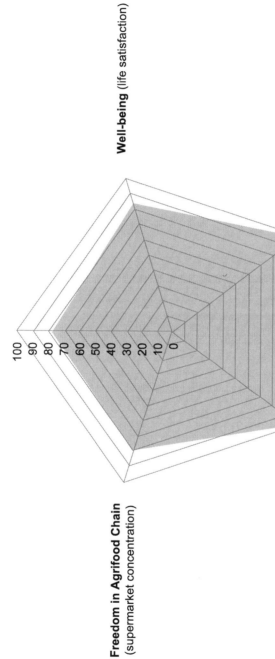

Figure 7.5 Costa Rica FHSI indices.

conventional understandings of food security to new variables, reflect an understanding that still deals in the currency of "things." While those things undoubtedly matter, I do not want readers to lose sight of the larger social milieu within which those states are embedded (see Figure 7.6). That milieu, it turns out, is of tremendous consequence to the process of food and human security. Also, by redirecting our gaze to this broader socio-economic environment, affluent nations start looking noticeably less food secure than when metrics like "calories produced per capita" or "disposable average household income spent on food" are used.

Take the concept of the "food desert" as an entry point into this discussion. Food deserts, for those unfamiliar with the term, are defined, at least according to the USDA, as urban neighborhoods and rural towns without ready access to fresh, healthy, and affordable food. Yet the concept of the food desert, I would argue, reflects an inability to see the general in the particular. Peter Berger (1963), in the classic sociological text *Invitation to Sociology*, speaks of the importance of seeing the general in the particular; of being able to grasp, in other words, the influence of higher-order influences, tendencies, and structural patterns in cases that might seem particular and unique. Food deserts, by nature of their very name, write off these instances of food insecurity as exceptions to the rule. The term "desert," after all, implies *absence*. As a sociologist, however, knowing how much general conditions—whether structures, policies, or ideologies—shape the particularities of place, I am uncomfortable with "exceptions to the rule" arguments. I cannot help but wonder if food deserts are less the exception to the rule and more *the rule itself*. For example, we know from the literature that some households have limited time to prepare healthy foods. Single parents working full time and taking care of children are particularly time poor, which can create an incentive for making food-purchasing decisions based in part on their convenience (Darmon and Drewnowski, 2008). Clearly, this growing body of research speaks to deeper *structural* problems that extend far beyond the household or even community level.

Pointing back to the issue of inequality and its role in making individuals, households, and nations more or less food secure, we know that the number of supermarkets that service low-income urban communities tend to be fewer compared to those in higher-income neighborhoods. In one study looking at Philadelphia, Pennsylvania, the highest-income neighborhoods had 156 percent more supermarkets

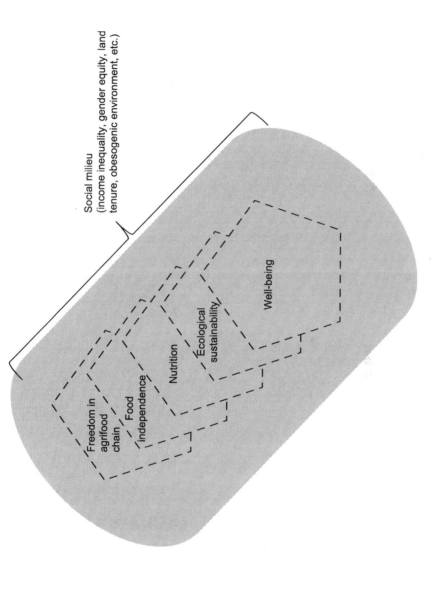

Social milieu (income inequality, gender equity, land tenure, obesogenic environment, etc.)

Freedom in agrifood chain

Food independence

Nutrition

Ecological sustainability

Well-being

Figure 7.6 Genuine food security.

than the lowest-income neighborhoods (Weinberg, 1995). Race also seems to matter in the US, as communities composed primarily of African Americans are found to, on average, have fewer supermarkets than those predominantly populated by residents of European descent, even after controlling for factors like neighborhood income (Powell et al., 2007). In Detroit, Michigan, the most impoverished African-American neighborhoods were found to be 1.1 miles farther from the closest supermarket compared to the most impoverished white neighborhoods. Compounding issues further, 28 percent of the residents in the low-income African-American communities studied did not own a car (Zenk et al., 2005). The literature is clear: food prices are higher, food quality poorer, and food selection more restricted in communities of high poverty compared to more affluent areas (Chung and Myers, 1999; Hendrickson et al., 2006).

Food access concerns are compounded by the lack of transportation, which is also tied up with issues of inequality. The distance of a mere couple of blocks might feel like much further to someone, for example, who is disabled and lacks the means to get to the store (and then carry their bulky purchases home). Low-income residents looking to shop at lower-priced supermarkets (due to greater competition) located outside of their immediate vicinity may have difficulty affording the additional cost of transportation, thereby limiting their food options to more local (and more expensive) outlets (Rose and Richards, 2004). Transportation to the nearest store is an even larger problem in rural areas, whether in the US, Northern Ireland, or the UK, where the nearest grocery store could be dozens of miles away (Furey et al., 2001; Shaw, 2006; USDA, 2009). In the US, some 2 million households live more than a mile from a supermarket and do not have a car or even access to one (USDA, 2009). Yet, even if one is perfectly able-bodied and the nearest store is close by, if the neighborhood is viewed as unsafe for walking, food access could remain a problem for households. Community safety levels have also been linked to the higher costs of food in urban areas, as higher rates of theft within urban stores have been found to drive up the cost of food items (Hendrickson et al., 2006).

Taking another step back, there remains a larger question: are the *environments* of affluent nations conducive to the process of genuine food security? This leads us to, among other things, the expansive literature on obesogenic (obesity-promoting) environments. An often-cited definition refers to an obesogenic environment as "the sum of influences that the surroundings, opportunities, or conditions of life have on promoting obesity in individuals or populations" (Swinburn and Egger, 2002, p. 289). Centuries ago, obesity may well have been flaunted as an indicator of high social status and personal food security. The rates of obesity that we are seeing today, however, carry an entirely different meaning. They are not, as one friend recently tried to tell me, "indicative of a nation that has mastered too well the food security puzzle."

Research on the obesogenic environment challenges conventional understandings of food security by highlighting yet another variable entirely ignored by myopic rhetoric around calories and cost: the built environment. In both the UK and the US, urban planning emerged in part out of a concern for the unsanitary urban conditions brought about by the rapid industrialization of cities in the nineteenth and early twentieth centuries. Laws about street widths and the presence of animals (which were increasingly pushed to the countryside) were thus developed with an eye toward improving sanitation and public hygiene. Yet, as the medical community developed more effective treatments for diseases and as waste-disposal techniques and technologies improved, the focus of urban planners began to shift. No longer needing to worry as much about the social and hygienic effects of their designs, they turned to the aesthetic and economic aspects of planning (Amelia and Townshend, 2006). In recent decades, urban planners and the medical health community have revived those channels of communication in recognition of the role that the built environment plays in terms of human health, individual and social levels of well-being, and, we can but hope, one day, food security (Northridge et al., 2003).

As noted previously, the food desert literature refers repeatedly to the role the built environment plays in restricting access to food choice. In practical terms, there is no difference between lacking access to spaces that offer a diverse selection of healthy and affordable food options and not having those spaces present in the first place. Perhaps not surprisingly, areas defined as food deserts also tend to be classified as obesogenic environments. For example, low-income individuals in Massachusetts who consumed fast food in the previous month had a mean BMI that was 2.4 kg/m^2 greater than low-income people who had better access to diverse food choices (Webb et al., 2008). In a study of women in California, obesity was more prevalent among the food insecure (31 percent) than among the food secure (16.2 percent) (Adams et al., 2003). And the link between food deserts and obesogenic environments does not appear to be confined to affluent nations. A study of rural households in Malaysia found rural women from food insecure households to be at a greater risk of obesity than rural women from food secure households (Shariff and Khor, 2005).

The mechanisms at work here are numerous. In some cases obesity is the result of a swinging pendulum between food sufficiency and food insecurity. Such feast–famine cycles have been linked to governmental food programs, which in some cases create periods of high-calorie intake (immediately after payment) followed by periods of involuntary food restriction when resources are not properly rationed (Dinour, 2007). This cycle has been known to be particularly detrimental to the health and well-being of mothers, as they frequently voluntarily restrict their own food intake during times of scarcity to ensure their children are sufficiently well fed (Webb et al., 2008).

We have seen repeatedly how affluence, in itself, does not contribute to food and human security, especially after a certain minimal threshold is reached. What seems to matter more is how that wealth is put to use. Affluent countries, for example, vary considerably in how they practice urban design. And these practices can be of tremendous consequence to their populations as a whole, irrespective of socioeconomic status. Figure 7.7 documents obesity rates and percent of total trips by walking, biking, or public transport for select affluent nations. Note the wide variation across high-income countries, due in no small part to the widely different built environments within these nations, or, in other words, due to how they choose to put their wealth to work.

Another tantalizing piece of supporting evidence for the argument that built environments are highly significant in promoting well-being is illustrated in Figure 7.8. Countries that encourage non-automobile forms of transportation—namely, walking, biking, and public transport—tend to score higher on the Happy Planet Index (HPI) than those that do not. To recall from Chapter 3, the HPI is a prosperity metric that takes into consideration a country's life expectancy at birth, general life satisfaction score, and ecological footprint. A high HPI score, in other words, reflects a society with high life expectancy, high life satisfaction, and low ecological footprint. While correlation is not the same as causation, there is ample evidence pointing to the fact that rising rates of societal auto-dependency negatively impact national levels of well-being while simultaneously increasing the size of its ecological footprint (Gärling, 2007; Portney, 2003).

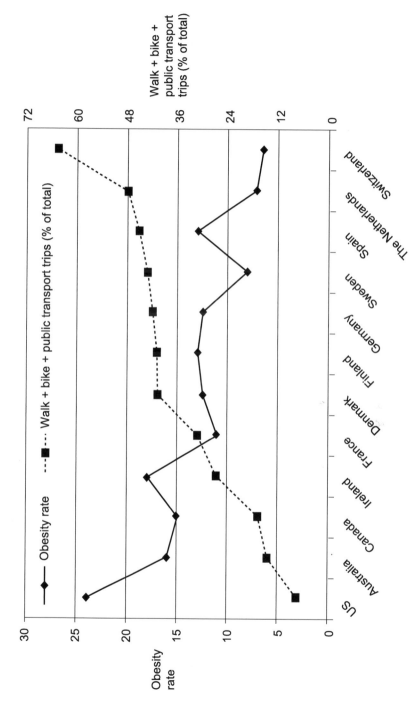

Figure 7.7 Obesity and percentage of total trips by walking, biking, or public transport for select affluent nations.

Source: Adapted from Bassett et al., 2008.

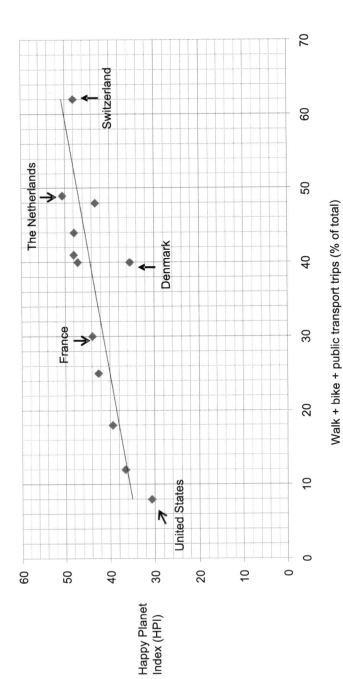

Figure 7.8 Link between Happy Planet Index and percentage of total trips by walking, biking, or public transport for select affluent nations.

It is also worth asking if a country that dumps billions of dollars annually into getting people to overconsume foods we know contribute to reduced well-being and welfare, creating a cycle that quickly becomes vicious, can be considered food secure. Altering consumption patterns in the direction of ever more empty calories further steers agrifood chains toward the production of these goods (along with all their environmental and human health "bads"), thereby further lowering their price, which in turn makes them even more attractive to price-sensitive consumers. A group of French researchers discovered that, after controlling for total caloric intake, a 100-gram increase in fats and sweets is associated with a 6–40-cent decrease in daily diet costs, while a 100-gram increase in fruits and vegetables is associated with a 22–35-cent increase in food expense (Maillot et al., 2007). A study looking at food items sold at major retail supermarket chains in Seattle, Washington, found nutrient density negatively associated with energy density and positively associated with cost (Monivais et al., 2010). The researchers note further that from 2004 to 2008 the price disparity between healthy and unhealthy foods grew, as "junk" food became cheaper and nutrient-dense foods more expensive. This supports the findings of an earlier study of Seattle-area supermarkets, noting that 25 cents' worth of cookies provides consumers with the same amount of energy as 95 cents' worth of carrots (Drewnowski and Specter, 2004).

Occasionally, when giving public lectures on food, I use props. Two of my favorites are a six-pack of Pop-Tarts and two red bell peppers. Why these items? Because they cost me about the same to purchase: roughly four dollars. This is truly a remarkable feat of the US food system. There are more than fifty different ingredients in a chocolate fudge Pop-Tart. A "Pop-Tart World" recently opened in Times Square, New York, joining the Hershey Store and M&M World at this internationally renowned location. And each pastry is a robust 200 kcal, making the entire four-dollar box a gut-busting 1,200 kcal. As for the two red bell peppers: one ingredient (the pepper itself); no "Red Bell Pepper World" (in fact, hardly any marketing campaign at all); and roughly 50 kcal each (that's assuming the peppers are large) or 100 kcal in total. Is it any surprise to learn that while the average American spends roughly 15 percent of their food budget on fruits and vegetables to meet government guidelines, that figure jumps to an unsustainable 70 percent among low-income households (Cassady et al., 2007)?

In addition to making certain foods incredibly inexpensive, we have created an environment—thanks in part to the empty calorie-ization of food security and the rise of FDI—that tells us we ought to be (over-)consuming those inexpensive calories. For every US dollar spent by the World Health Organization on preventing diseases caused by Western diets, more than US$500 is spent by the food industry promoting those diets. In the UK, the government spends £5 million annually on nutritional educational campaigns; Coca-Cola alone spends £27 million on advertising to UK consumers (Land and Heasman, 2004). Or take the US$4.2 *billion* spent annually by the fast-food industry in the US. To put that figure into some perspective, consider the annual budget of the Center for Nutrition Policy and Promotion (the USDA's sub-agency charged with improving the health and well-being of Americans): US$6.5 *million* (Philpott, 2010).

The great twentieth-century economist John Kenneth Galbraith referred to the rise of marketing and advertising as leading to "the revised sequence." Rather than satisfying the wants and demands of the consumer, the modern firm (agrifood included) "accommodates the consumer to the goals of the technostructure and provides a climate of social belief that is favorable to this result" (Galbraith, 1967, p. 235). Galbraith's point is that firms survive today by convincing people to want what they sell, rather than reactively supplying what people want. The empirical evidence certainly seems to support this conclusion.

A recent study featured on the website of the venerable American Academy of Pediatrics involved a US sample of 3,342 individuals aged between fifteen and twenty-three (AAP, 2012). In addition to asking the participants a variety of questions about demographics and personal eating, exercise, and television viewing habits, the researchers showed them twenty still images from television ads for well-known fast-food restaurants that had aired in the year before the survey. All of the images were digitally edited to remove the brands. The participants were then asked if they remembered seeing the advertisement, if they liked it, and if they could name the brand. Roughly 18 percent of the participants were overweight and 15 percent were obese. The percentage of youths who were obese was significantly higher among those who recognized more ads than among those who recognized few—17 percent versus 8.3 percent. Even after controlling for a variety of demographic and personal-habit variables (e.g., time spent watching television, frequency of exercise, sanitary level, etc.), youths who recognized many ads were more than twice as likely to be obese compared with those who recognized just a few.

The following stunning admission is taken from an article by Rory Sutherland (2010), vice-chairman of marketing firm Ogilvy UK and at the time president of the Institute of Practitioners in Advertising:

> The truth is that marketing raises enormous ethical questions every day—at least it does if you're doing it right. If this were not the case, the only possible explanations are either that you believe marketers are too ineffectual to make any difference, or you believe that marketing activities only affect people at the level of conscious argument. Neither of these possibilities appeals to me. *I would rather be thought of as evil than useless.*
>
> (Sutherland, 2010, p. 59; my emphasis)

Decades of studies note how advertising promotes rabid consumerism (see, e.g., Galbraith, 1958). That is, after all, one of the precursors to economic growth: the ability to create insatiable needs. As Ezra Mishan (1967, p. 149), long-time Professor of Economics at the London School of Economics, famously noted half a century ago: "Therefore to continue to regard the market, in an affluent and growing economy, as primarily a 'want-satisfying' mechanism is to close one's eyes to the more important fact, that it has become a want-*creating* mechanism" (emphasis in original). We also know that advertising reinforces the values it reflects by "normalizing" them. On this point, talking specifically about smoking, Rory Sutherland (2010, p. 59) further confessed: "While I can accept that the purpose of tobacco advertising was not to encourage people to smoke, I find it astounding that anyone could barefacedly suggest that cigarette posters seen everywhere did not serve to normalise the habit."

There is some talk of replacing the term "food desert" with "food swamp" (USDA, 2009). The former highlights the lack of healthy food options in a particular space, while the latter emphasizes the abundance of less healthy food options (Rose et al., 2009). Yet, I think "food swamp" still misses the mark. I prefer an alternative (ecosystem) metaphor: food *oceans*. Picture a person stranded on an open sea. Our fictitious individual, lying in their life raft, baking under the sun, is paradoxically dying of thirst, even though they are surrounded by copious amounts of water. They could drink the sea water but that would only hasten their demise as their kidneys buckled from the duress of having to process all the salt (which would then only make them thirstier). Not all water is the same. The same is true of food. Sure, we can feast all we want on cheap, empty calories. Yet such a diet comes with a cost. As illustrated empirically in earlier chapters, living on "cheap food"—the items that modern agrifood systems have become really proficient at producing—exacts a serious toll on one's body and overall human and planetary wellbeing. And this "ocean" is truly like an ecosystem in places like the US, where phenomena akin to feedback mechanisms (e.g., advertisement, marketing, and investment sectors) are in place to perpetuate its existence.

Towards a new social imaginary

Like others, I have become highly critical of the direction in which we have been led under the banner of "food security." Yet, if we can keep in mind the term's roots, which extend back at least as far as to Roosevelt's 1941 State of the Union address, we find that the term itself is not the problem. Rather, the problem has been in its application. By employing the term, I am seeking to recapture the original spirit of food security that has been lost; a spirit, I might add, that haunts certain movements that are presently critical of policies promoted in its name. In its position statement, *Food Sovereignty: A Future without Hunger*, La Via Campesina states: "Food sovereignty is the right of each nation to maintain and develop its own capacity to produce its basic foods respecting cultural and productive diversity. We have the right to produce our own food in our own territory. Food sovereignty is a precondition to *genuine food security*" (La Via Campesina, 1996, p. 1; my emphasis). It seems that even those who are highly critical of the term, and who are looking to supplant it with something else, are always drawn back to it. I too feel its pull. In keeping with Roosevelt's "four freedoms" speech, genuine food security is about promoting freedom with the ultimate aim of enhancing human welfare (which presupposes such rights as social justice, human health, and ecological sustainability). That is something I can get behind.

If we are truly interested in making people better off, then it is time to reevaluate what we have done up to this point in the name of food security. In some respects, the last fifty-plus years have been a grand experiment. But now the time has come to evaluate the outcomes of this project empirically. We have certainly given it plenty of opportunities (some might say too many) to show its merit. That, essentially, is what this book attempts to do. The findings are sobering. While we produce more calories globally now than we have ever produced before, we are heading, according to too many metrics to list here, in a direction that looks to be anything but food secure—unless, that is, you methodologically reduce food security to calorie production.

The philosopher Charles Taylor (2004) has written a remarkably lucid account of what he calls "modern social imaginaries" in a book of the same title. He describes how a "new conception of moral order" has come to grip Western societies. It began, according to Taylor, as "just an idea in the minds of some influential thinkers, but it later came to shape the social imaginary of large strata, and then eventually whole societies," where it is now "self-evident" (p. 2). Taylor is writing of the rise of a distinct political moral order, not about food security. But I see overlap between his idea of social imaginaries and what I have written about here. We seem to be locked into a food security imaginary that is inherently bound up with arguments about the "need" to produce more food. Yet when that becomes *the* starting point of discussion it directs attention away from some important questions. *Why* do we think we need to produce more food in the first place? And at *what* and *whose* expense are we willing to achieve these gains in productivity? For example, the unforgivable amount of food we currently waste is one reason why we *think* we need to produce more. By leaving those "needs" unexamined, and building into our future food estimates all that waste, we are only making the task at hand all the more difficult.

We also need a social imaginary that treats food differently from other commodities. As described by the twentieth-century historian E.P. Thompson (1971), there was, in the sixteenth and seventeenth centuries, an "old moral economy" of provision that emphasized the common well-being of society and placed limits on the market. In this economy, millers, bakers, and other merchants involved in the British food system were "considered as servants of the community, working not for a profit but for fair allowance" (p. 83). This is certainly an aim that would today enhance individual and social liberties in light of the tremendous concentration and market distortions that plague so-called modern agrifood chains.

As the previous pages detail, affluence, productivism, free trade, and growth do not automatically guarantee those things that ultimately matter to us as humans nor are they necessary for the survival of humanity. The grand experiment I mentioned earlier involved the "breakthrough of the new political economy of the free market . . . [and] the breakdown of the old moral economy of provision" (Thompson, 1971, p. 136). That experiment has not made the world more food secure. The old moral economy was predicated upon care first and economics second. Perhaps if we started to care again about those things that really matter to us, we would have a better shot at achieving our goal of reclaiming genuine food security.

References

AAP (2012) Familiarity with television fast-food ads linked to obesity, *American Academy of Pediatrics*, April 29, http://www.aap.org/en-us/about-the-aap/aap-press-room/pages/Familiarity-With-Television-Fast-Food-Ads-Linked-to-Obesity.aspx?nfstatus=401&nftoken=00000000-0000-0000-0000-000000000000&nfstatusdescription=ERROR%3a+No+local+token, last accessed July 16, 2012.

Achard, F., H. Eva, H.-J. Stibig, P. Mayaux, J. Gallego, T. Richards, and J.-P. Malingreau (2002) Determination of deforest rates of the world's tropical forests, *Science*, 297(5583), pp. 999–1002.

Adams, D. and M. Salois (2010) Local versus organic: A turn in consumer preferences and willingness-to-pay, *Renewable Agriculture and Food Systems*, 25(4), pp. 331–341.

Adams, Elizabeth, Laurence Grummer-Strawn, and Gilberto Chavez (2003) Food insecurity is associated with increased risk of obesity in California women, *Journal of Nutrition*, 133(4), pp. 1070–1074.

Agarwal, B. (1994) *A Field of One's Own: Gender and Land Rights in South Asia*. Cambridge: Cambridge University Press.

Agarwal, B. (2010) *Gender and Green Governance: The Political Economy of Women's Presence within and beyond Community Forestry*. New York and Oxford: Oxford University Press.

Agarwal, B. (2011) Food crises and gender inequality, DESA Working Paper No. 107, United Nations, June, http://www.un.org/esa/desa/papers/2011/wp107_2011.pdf, last accessed July 15, 2012.

Agarwal, B. and P. Panda (2007) Toward freedom from domestic violence: The neglected obvious, *Journal of Human Development*, 8(3), pp. 359–388.

Alexander, William (2008) *Resiliency in Hostile Environments: A Comunidad Agricola in Chile's Norte Chico*. Cranbury, NY: Rosemount.

Alkon, A. and J. Agyeman (eds) (2011) *Cultivating Food Justice: Race, Class, and Sustainability*. Cambridge, MA: MIT Press.

Allen, P. and J. Guthman (2006) From "old school" to "Farm to School": Neoliberalization from the ground up, *Agriculture and Human Values*, 23(4), pp. 401–415.

Almas, R. and H. Campbell (2012) *Rethinking Agricultural Policy Regimes: Food Security, Climate Change, and the Future Resilience of Global Agriculture*. Bingley: Emerald.

Altieri, Miguel (1999) Applying agroecology to enhance the productivity of peasant farming systems in Latin America, *Environment, Development and Sustainability*, 1, pp. 197–217.

Altieri, Miguel (2004) *Biodiversity and Pest Management in Agroecosystems*. Binghamton, NY: Food Products Press.

Altieri, Miguel and Clara Nicholls (2008) Scaling up agroecological approaches for food sovereignty in Latin America, *Development*, 51(4), pp. 472–480.

Amelia, L. and T. Townshend (2006) Obesogenic environments: Exploring the built and food environments, *Journal of the Royal Society for the Promotion of Health*, 126(6), pp. 262–267.

Anders, S. (2008) Imperfect competition in German food retailing: Evidence from state level data, *Atlantic Economic Journal*, 36(4), pp. 441–454.

Anderson, T.L. (2004) Why economic growth is good for the environment, *Hoover Digest*, 3, http://www.perc.org/articles/article446.php, last accessed October 16, 2012.

Armsby, H. (1911) The conservation of the food supply, *Popular Science*, 79, pp. 469–501.

Arroyo, P., A. Loria, and O. Mendez (2004) Changes in the household calorie supply during the 1994 economic crisis in Mexico and its implications for the obesity epidemic, *Nutrition Reviews*, 62, pp. S163–S168.

Babu, C. and A. Gulati (eds) (2005) *Economic Reforms and Food Security*. Binghamton, NY: Food Products Press.

Badgley, C., J. Moghtader, E. Quintero, E. Zakem, M. Chappell, K. Aviles-Vazquez, A. Samulon, and I. Perfecto (2007) Organic agriculture and the global food supply, *Renewable Agriculture and Food Systems*, 22, pp. 86–108.

Ball, Kylie, David Crawford, and Justin Kenardy (2004) Longitudinal relationships among overweight, life satisfaction, and aspirations in young women, *Obesity*, 12(6), pp. 1019–1030.

Barham, A., B. Barham, A. Johnson, D. Allen, J. Blanton, and M. Miller (2002) Effects of the transportation of beef cattle from the feedyard to the packing plant on prevalence levels of *Escherichia coli* O157 and *Salmonella* spp', *Journal of Food Protection*, 65, pp. 280–283.

Barr, Diana (2012) Monsanto see Q4 loss widen to $219 million, *St. Louis Business Journal*, October 3, http://www.bizjournals.com/stlouis/news/2012/10/03/monsanto-sees-q4-loss-widen.html, last accessed October 21, 2012.

Bassett, D., J. Pucher, R. Buehler, D.L. Thompson, and S.E. Crouter (2008) Walking, cycling, and obesity rates in Europe, North America, and Australia, *Journal of Physical Activity and Health*, 5, pp. 795–814.

Bates, B., Z. Kundzewicz, S. Wu, and J. Palutikof (eds) (2008) Climate change and water, White Paper, Intergovernmental Panel on Climate Change, Geneva, http://www.ipcc.ch/pdf/technical-papers/ccw/frontmatter.pdf, last accessed June 29, 2012.

Battisti, D. and R. Naylor (2009) Historical warning of future food insecurity, *Science*, 323, pp. 240–244.

Baylies, C. (2002) The impact of AIDS on rural households in Africa: A shock like any other?, *Development and Change*, 33(4), pp. 611–632.

Bellarby, J., B. Foereid, A. Hastings, and P. Smith (2008) *Cool Farming: Climate Impacts of Agriculture and Mitigation Potential*. Amsterdam: Greenpeace International.

Bello, W. (2008) How to manufacture a food crisis, *Development*, 51(4), pp. 450–455.

Berger, P. (1963) *Invitation to Sociology: A Humanist Perspective*. New York: Anchor.

Bezemer, Dirk and Derek Headey (2008) Agriculture, development and urban bias, *World Development*, 36(8), pp. 1342–1364.

Blanchard, T. and Matthews, T. (2008) Retail concentration, food deserts, and food disadvantaged communities in rural America, in C. Hinrichs and T. Lyson (eds) *Remaking the North American Food System: Strategies for Sustainability*. Lincoln: University of Nebraska Press, pp. 201–215.

Blas, J. (2010) End looms for fertiliser cartels, *Financial Times*, August 19, http://www.ft.com/cms/s/0/dd65a148-abb4–11df-9f02–00144feabdc0. html#axzz1zyVQDtoJ, last accessed July 10, 2012.

Bloomberg (2009) Wal-Mart's store-brand groceries to get new emphasis, February 19, http://www.bloomberg.com/apps/news?sid=afVJJxZ4oCtY &pid=newsarchive, last accessed July 9, 2012.

Bomford, M. (2011) Beyond food miles, Post Carbon Institute, Santa Rosa, CA, March 9, http://www.postcarbon.org/article/273686-beyond-food-miles#_edn9, last accessed April 12, 2011.

Burch, D. and G. Lawrence (2007) Supermarket own brands, new foods and the reconfiguration of agri-food supply chains, in D. Burch and G. Lawrence (eds) *Supermarkets and Agri-Food Supply Chains: Transformations in the Production and Consumption of Foods*. Northampton, MA: Edward Elgar, pp. 100–128.

Burch, D. and G. Lawrence (eds) (2007) *Supermarkets and Agri-Food Supply Chains*. Northampton, MA: Edward Elgar.

Busch, L. (2010) Can fairy tales come true? The surprising story of neoliberalism and world agriculture, *Sociologia Ruralis*, 50(4), pp. 331–351.

Buttel, F. (2005) Ever since Hightower: The politics of agricultural research activism in the molecular age, *Agriculture and Human Values*, 22(3), pp. 275–283.

Camporesi, P. (1989) *Bread of Dreams: Food Fantasy in Early Modern Europe*. Chicago, IL: University of Chicago Press.

Canning, P., A. Charles, S. Huang, K. Polenske, and A. Waters (2010) Energy use in the US food system, United States Department of Agriculture, Economic Research Service, Report No. 94, March, Washington, DC, http://ddr.nal.usda.gov/bitstream/10113/41413/1/CAT31049057.pdf, last accessed January 1, 2012.

Carolan, M. (2009) The costs and benefits of biofuels: A review of recent peer-reviewed research and a sociological look ahead, *Environmental Practice*, 11, pp. 17–24.

Carolan, M. (2010) Ethanol's most recent breakthrough in the United States: A case of socio-technical transition, *Technology in Society*, 32(2), pp. 65–71.

Carolan, M. (2011a) *Embodied Food Politics*. Burlington, VT: Ashgate.

Carolan, M. (2011b) *The Real Cost of Cheap Food*. New York: Earthscan.

Carolan, M. (2012) The Food and Human Security Index: Rethinking food security and "growth", *International Journal of Sociology of Agriculture and Food*, 19(2), pp. 176–200.

Cassady, D., K. Jetter, and J. Culp (2007) Is price a barrier to eating more fruits and vegetables for low income families?, *Journal of the American Dietetic Association*, 107(11), pp. 1909–1915.

Catel, P. (2011) *Raising Livestock*. Chicago: Heinemann-Raintree.

CDC (2010) 2009 H1N1 flu: Situation update, http://www.cdc.gov/h1n1flu/update.htm, last accessed July 14, 2012.

CDC (nd) Adult obesity facts, http://www.cdc.gov/obesity/data/adult.html, last accessed August 18, 2012.

Chapagain, A. and A. Hoekstra (2003) Virtual water flows between nations in relation to trade in livestock and livestock products, Research Report Series No. 13, UNESCO-IHE, Delf, Netherlands, http://www.waterfootprint.org/Reports/Report13.pdf, last accessed June 30, 2012.

Christen, K. (2007) Closing the phosphorus loop, *Environmental Science and Technology*, April 1, p. 2078.

Chung, C. and S. Myers (1999) Do the poor pay more for food? An analysis of grocery store availability and food price disparities, *Journal of Consumer Affairs*, 33(2), pp. 276–296.

Clark, S., C. Hawkes, S. Murphy, K. Hansen-Kuhn, and D. Wallinga (2012) Exporting obesity: US farm and trade policy and the transformation of the Mexican consumer food environment, *International Journal of Occupational and Environmental Health*, 18(1), pp. 53–65.

Clay, J. (2011) Freeze the footprint of food, *Nature*, 475, pp. 287–289.

Cleaver, H. (1972) The contradictions of the green revolution, *American Economic Review*, 62(1/2), pp. 177–186.

Cochrane, W. (1993) *The Development of American Agriculture: A Historical Analysis*. Minneapolis: University of Minnesota Press.

Cooper, J. and H. Dobson (2007) The benefits of pesticides to mankind and the environment, *Crop Protection*, 26(9), pp. 1337–1348.

Cordain, L. (1999) Cereal grains: Humanity's double-edged sword, *World Review of Nutrition and Dietetics*, 84, pp. 19–23.

Cotterill, R. (2006) Antitrust analysis of supermarkets: Global concerns playing out in local markets, *Australian Journal of Agricultural and Resource Economics*, 50(1), pp. 17–32.

Council on Foreign Relations (2005) Council on Foreign Relations Conference on the Global Threat of Pandemic Influenza, Session 1: Avian flu – where do we stand?, Transcript, http://www.cfr.org/publication /9230/council_on_foreign_relations_conference_on_the_global_threat_ of_pandemic_influenza_session_1.html, last accessed July 14, 2012.

Cunha, L. (2009) Water: A human right or an economic resource?, in M. Ramón Llamas, L. Martínez-Cortina, and A. Mukherji (eds) *Water Ethics*. Boca Raton, FL: CRC Press, pp. 97–113.

Cutler, D., E. Glaeser, and J. Shapiro (2003) Why have Americans become more obese?, *Journal of Economic Perspectives*, 17(3), pp. 93–118.

Daly, H. (1996) *Beyond Growth: The Economics of Sustainable Development*. Boston, MA: Beacon Press.

Daly, H. (1999) *Ecological Economics and the Ecology of Economics*. Northhampton, MA: Edward Elgar.

Darmon, N. and A. Drewnowski (2008) Does social class predict diet quality?, *American Journal of Clinical Nutrition*, 87, pp. 1107–1117.

Davis, M. (2001) *Late Victorian Holocausts: El Niño Famines and the Making of the Third World*. London: Verso.

de Fraiture, C., X. Cai, U. Amarasinghe, M. Rosegrant, and D. Molden (2004) Does international cereal trade save water? The impact of virtual water trade on global water use, Comprehensive Assessment of Water Management in Agriculture Research Report No. 4, International Water Management Institute, Colombo, Sri Lanka, http://www.iwmi.cgiar.org/Assessment/ FILES/pdf/publications/ResearchReports/CARRl4.pdf, last accessed June 30, 2012.

de Janvry, A. and E. Sadoulet (1989) A study in resistance to institutional change: The lost game of Latin American reform, *World Development*, 17(9), pp. 1397–1407.

DeLind, L. (2006) Of bodies, place and culture: Re-situating local food, *Journal of Agricultural and Environmental Ethics*, 19(1), pp. 121–146.

Desrochers, P. and H. Shimizu (2008) Yes, we have no bananas: A critique of the "food miles" perspective, Policy Primer No. 8, Mercatus Center, George Mason University, Washington, DC.

de Vries, F., H. Acquay, D. Molden, S. Scherr, C. Valentin, and O. Cofie (2008) Learning from bright spots to enhance food security and to combat degradation of water and land resources, in D. Bossio and K. Geheb (eds) *Conserving Land, Protecting Water*. Wallingford: CABI, pp. 1–19.

Dietz, T., E. Rosa, and R. York (2012) Environmentally efficient well-being: Is there a Kuznets curve?, *Environmental Geography*, 32, pp. 21–28.

Dimitri, C., A. Tegene, and P. Kaufman (2003) US fresh produce markets: Marketing channels, trade practices, and retail pricing behavior, Agricultural Economic Report No. 825, September, http://www.ers.usda.gov/Publications/AER825, last accessed July 9, 2012.

Dinour, L. (2007) The food insecurity–obesity paradox: A review of the literature and the role food stamps may play, *Journal of the American Dietetic Association*, 107(11), pp. 1952–1961.

Dixon, H. and D. Broom (2007) *The Seven Deadly Sins of Obesity*. Sydney: UNSW Press.

Domina, D. and C.R. Taylor (2009) The debilitating effects of concentration in markets affecting agriculture, Organization for Competitive Markets, October 5, http://www.farmfutures.com/mdfm/Faress1/author/2/OCM%20competition%20report.Pdf, last accessed October 14, 2012.

Domina, D. and C.R. Taylor (2010) The debilitating effects of concentration markets affecting agriculture, *Drake Journal of Agricultural Law*, 15(1), pp. 61–108.

Donham, K. (2010) Community and occupational health concerns in pork production: A review, *Journal of Animal Science*, 88, pp. 102–111.

Donham, K. and A. Thelin (2006) *Agricultural Medicine: Occupational and Environmental Health for the Health Professions*, Oxford: Blackwell.

Donham, K., S. Wing, D. Osterberg, J. Flora, C. Hodne, K. Thu, and P. Thorne (2007) Community health and socioeconomic issues surrounding concentrated animal feeding operations, *Environmental Health Perspectives*, 115(2), pp. 317–320.

Donovan, C., L. Bailey, E. Mpyisi, and M. Weber (2003) Prime-age adult morbidity and mortality in rural Rwanda: Effects on household income, agricultural production, and food security strategies, research report for Ministry of Agriculture, Livestock, and Forestry, March, http://www.aec.msu.edu/fs2/rwanda/RLDS3_2003.pdf, last accessed July 27, 2012.

Doss, C. (2011) If women hold up half the sky, how much of the world's food do they produce?, Food and Agriculture Organization of the United Nations, Working Paper No. 11–14, March, Rome, http://www.research-nest.com/all_reports/13073410251am309e00.pdf, last accessed July 15, 2012.

Drewnowski, A. and N. Darmon (2005a) Food choices and diet costs: An economic analysis, *Journal of Nutrition*, 135(4), pp. 900–904.

Drewnowski, A. and N. Darmon (2005b) The economics of obesity: Dietary energy density and energy cost, *American Journal of Clinical Nutrition*, 82(1), pp. 265S–273S.

Drewnowski, A. and S. Specter (2004) Poverty and obesity: The role of energy density and energy costs, *American Journal of Clinical Nutrition*, 79(1), pp. 6–16.

D'Silva, J. and J. Webster (eds) (2010) *The Meat Crisis: Developing More Sustainable Production and Consumption*. London: Earthscan.

Dumke, N. (2005) The hunger–obesity paradox, *Journal of the National Medical Association*, 97(12), p. 1651.

Dutta, Indranil and Craig Gundersen (2007) Measures of food insecurity at the household level, in Basudeb Guha-Khasnobis, Shabd Acharya, and Benjamin Davis (eds) *Food Security*. New York: Oxford University Press, pp. 42–61.

Dyer, J. and R. Desjardins (2003) The impact of farm machinery management on the greenhouse gas emissions from Canadian agriculture, *Journal of Sustainable Agriculture*, 22(3), pp. 59–74.

Eckholm, E. (2010) US meat farmers brace for limits on antibiotics, *New York Times*, September 14, http://www.nytimes.com/2010/09/15/us/15farm.html, last accessed July 10, 2012.

Eliot, M. and M. Heseltine (1937) Nutrition studies of the League of Nations and the International Labour Office Geneva, *Social Service Review*, 11(2), pp. 331–334.

Ellis, Frank (2005) Small farms, livelihood diversification, and rural–urban transitions: Strategic issues in Sub-Saharan Africa, in *The Future of Small Farms: Proceedings of a Research Workshop*, organized by International Food Policy Research Institute and Overseas Development Institute, Imperial College, London, http://citeseerx. ist.psu.edu/viewdoc/download?doi=10.1.1.139.3719&rep=rep1&type=pdf#page=142, last accessed March 25, 2012.

Emerson, J., D. Esty, M. Levy, C. Kim, V. Mara, A. de Sherbinin, and T. Srebotnjak (2010) *2010 Environmental Performance Index*. New Haven, CT: Yale Center for Environmental Law and Policy.

ETC Group (2008) Who owns nature? Corporate power and the final frontier in the commodification of life, http://www.etcgroup.org/upload/publication/707/01/etc_won_report_final_color.pdf, last accessed July 10, 2012.

Fan, Shenggen, P. Hazell, and S. Sukhadeo Thorat (2000) Government spending, growth and poverty in rural India, *American Journal of Agricultural Economics*, 82(4), pp. 1038–1051.

FAO (1943) *United Nations Conference on Food and Agriculture: Hot Springs, Virginia, May 18–June 3, Final Acts and Section Reports*, Washington, DC: United States Government Printing Office.

FAO (2002) Reducing poverty and hunger: The critical role of financing for food, agriculture and rural development, Food and Agriculture

Organization, World Food Programme, Rome, ftp://ftp.fao.org/docrep/fao/003/Y6265E/Y6265E.pdf, last accessed August 18, 2012.

FAO (2008) Climate change and food security, Food and Agriculture Organization of the United Nations, Rome, http://www.fao.org/forestry/15538-079b31d45081fe9c3dbc6ff34de4807e4.pdf, last accessed March 25, 2012.

FAO (2011) World Hunger Report 2011: High, volatile prices set to continue, Media Center, Food and Agriculture Organization, Rome, http://www.fao.org/news/story/en/item/92495/icode/, last accessed August 18, 2012.

FAO (2012) Road to Rio: Improving energy use key challenge for world's food systems, Food and Agriculture Organization of the United Nations, Rome, http://www.fao.org/news/story/en/item/146971/icode/, last accessed June 24, 2012.

FAO (nd) Hunger statistics, World Food Programme, Food and Agriculture Organization of the United Nations, Rome, http://www.wfp.org/hunger/stats, last accessed August 18, 2012.

Farina, E. (2001) Challenges for Brazil's food industry in the context of globalization and Mercosur consolidation, *International Food and Agribusiness Management Review*, 2, pp. 315–330.

Finkelstein, E. and L. Zuckerman (2008) *The Fattening of America: How the Economy Makes Us Fat, if It Matters, and What to Do about It.* Hoboken, NJ: Wiley.

Fischer, G., F. Tubiello, H. van Velthuizen, and D. Wiberg (2006) Climate change impacts on irrigation water requirements: Effects of mitigation, 1990/2080, *Technology Forecasting and Social Change*, 74, pp. 1083–1107.

Foer, A. (2010) *Agriculture and Antitrust Enforcement Issues in Our 21st Century Economy, Proceedings of the December 8, 2010 Workshop*, Washington, DC: US Department of Agriculture and Department of Justice, http://www.justice.gov/atr/public/workshops/ag2010/dc-agworkshop-tran-script.pdf, last accessed July 8, 2012, pp. 219–252.

Food and Water Watch (2012) Why Walmart can't fix the food system, Washington, DC, http://documents.foodandwaterwatch.org/doc/FoodandWaterWatchReportWalmart022112.pdf, last accessed July 19, 2012.

Fox, M., S. Rosen, W. MacLeod, M. Wasunna, M. Bii, G. Foglia, and J. Simon (2004) The impact of HIV/AIDS on labour productivity in Kenya, *Tropical Medicine and International Health*, 9, pp. 318–324.

Freebairn, D. (1995) Did the green revolution concentrate incomes? A quantitative study of research reports, *World Development*, 23(2), pp. 265–279.

Friedmann, H. (1990) The origins of third world food dependence, in H. Bernstein, B. Crow, M. Mackintosh, and C. Martin (eds) *The Food*

Question: Profits versus People. New York: Monthly Review Press, pp. 13–31.

Friedmann, H. (1992) Distance and durability: Shaky foundations of the world food economy, *Third World Quarterly*, 13(2), pp. 371–383.

Friends of the Earth (2010) Healthy planet eating: How lower meat diets can save lives and the planet, http://www.foe.co.uk/resource/reports/healthy_planet_eating.pdf, last accessed January 4, 2012.

Furey, S., C. Strugnell, and H. McIlveen (2001) An investigation of the potential existence of "food deserts" in rural and urban areas of Northern Ireland, *Agriculture and Human Values*, 18, pp. 447–457.

Galbraith, J.K. (1958) *The Affluent Society*. New York: Penguin.

Galbraith, J.K. (1967) *The New Industrial State*. Harmondsworth: Penguin.

GAO (2012) Food safety: FDA's food advisory and recall process needs strengthening, Report to Congressional Committees GAO-12–589, July, US Government Accountability Office, Washington, DC, http://www.gao.gov/assets/600/593031.pdf, last accessed August 9, 2012.

Gärling, T. (2007) *Threats from Car Traffic to the Quality of Urban Life*. Amsterdam: Elsevier.

Garming, H. and H. Waibel (2009) Pesticides and farmer health in Nicaragua: A willingness-to-pay approach to evaluation, *European Journal of Health Economics*, 10(2), pp. 125–133.

Gilding, P. (2011) *The Great Disruption*. New York: Bloomsbury Press.

Gkogka, E., M. Reij, A. Havelaar, M. Zwietering, and L. Gorris (2011) Risk-based estimate of effect of foodborne disease on public health, Greece, *Emerging Infectious Diseases*, 17(9), http://dx.doi.org/10.3201/eid1709.101766, last accessed October 14, 2012.

Gliessman, S. (1998) *Agroecology: Ecological Process in Sustainable Agriculture*. Ann Arbor, MI: Ann Arbor Press.

Gonzalez, C. (2004) Trade liberalization, food security, and the environment: The neoliberal threat to sustainable rural development, *Transnational Law and Contemporary Problems*, 14, pp. 419–498.

Gooch, M., A. Felfel, and N. Marenick (2010) Food waste in Canada, George Morris Center, University of Guelph, Guelph, Canada, http://www.vcmtools.ca/pdf/Food%20Waste%20in%20Canada%20120910.pdf, last accessed March 16, 2012.

Gottlieb, R. (2010) *Food Justice*. Cambridge, MA: MIT Press.

Grazer, W. (2005) *Terrors at the Table: The Curious History of Nutrition*. New York: Oxford University Press.

Gupta, R. and A. Seth (2007) A review of resource conserving technologies for sustainable management of the wheat-cropping systems of the Indo-Gangetic Plains (IGP), *Crop Production*, 26(3), pp. 436–447.

Gustavsson, J., R. Otterdijk, and A. Meybeck (2011) Global food losses and food waste, Food and Agriculture Organization of the

United Nations, Rome, http://www.fao.org/docrep/014/mb060e/mb060e00.pdf, last accessed July 2, 2012.

Guthman, J. (2011) *Weighing In: Obesity, Food Justice and the Limits of Capitalism*. Los Angeles: University of California Press.

Haq, M. (1995) *Reflections on Human Development*. New York: Oxford University Press.

Harris, J., J. Bargh, and K. Brownell (2009) Priming effects of television food advertising on eating behavior, *Health Psychology*, 28(4), pp. 404–413.

Harvey, D. (2005) *Brief History of Neoliberalism*. New York: Oxford University Press.

Harvey, J., M. Hendrickson, and P. Howard (2012) Networks, power and dependency in the agrifood industry, working paper, February, Department of Agricultural Economics, University of Missouri, Columbia, MO.

Hauter, W. (2009) Agriculture and antitrust enforcement issues in our 21st century economy, comments submitted to the US Department of Justice and US Department of Agriculture on Agriculture and Antitrust Enforcement Issues in Our 21st Century Economy (74 Fed. Reg. 165 43725–43726), Food and Water Watch Institute, Washington, DC, December 31.

Hawkes, C. (2005) The role of foreign direct investment in the nutrition transition, *Public Health Nutrition*, 8(4), pp. 357–365.

Hawkes, C. (2008) Dietary implications of supermarket development: A global perspective, *Development Policy Review*, 26(6), pp. 657–692.

Hendrickson, D., C. Smith, and N. Eikenberry (2006) Fruit and vegetable access in four low-income food desert communities in Minnesota, *Agriculture and Human Values*, 23, pp. 371–383.

Hendrickson, M. and W. Heffernan (2007) Concentration of agricultural markets, Department of Rural Sociology, University of Missouri, Columbia, http://www.foodcircles.missouri.edu/07contable.pdf, last accessed October 21, 2012.

Hishaw, J. (2007) Show me no rice pharming: An overview of the introduction of and opposition to genetically engineered pharmaceutical crops in the United States, *Journal of Food Law and Policy*, 3, pp. 209–227.

Hoekstra, A., A. Chapagain, M. Aldaya, and M. Mekonnen (2011) *The Water Footprint Assessment Manual: Setting the Global Standard*. London: Earthscan.

Howard, Philip (2009) Visualizing consolidation in the global seed industry: 1996–2008, *Sustainability*, 1, pp. 1266–1287.

Hurst, D. (2010) Growers go bananas over waste, *Brisbane Times*, January 7, http://www.brisbanetimes.com.au/business/growers-go-bananas-over-waste-20100106-lu7q.html, last accessed March 30, 2012.

Ilbery, B. (2012) Interrogating food security and infectious animal and plant diseases: A critical introduction, *Geographical Journal*, 178(4), pp. 308–312.

Inderset, R. and T. Valletti (2011) Buyer power and the "waterbed effect", *Journal of Industrial Economics*, 59(1), pp. 1–20.

InterAcademy Council (2003) Realising the promise and potential of African agriculture: Science and technology strategies for improving agricultural productivity and food security in Africa, http://www.cgiar.org/pdf/agm04/agm04_iacpanel_execsumm.pdf, last accessed August 8, 2012.

IPCC (2007) *Climate Change 2007: Mitigation of Climate Change*. Cambridge: Cambridge University Press.

IPS (2008) Executive excess 2008: How average taxpayers subsidize runaway pay, http:///www.faireconomy.org/files/executive_excess_2008.pdf, last accessed April 28, 2012.

Jackson, T. (2009) *Prosperity without Growth*. London: Earthscan.

Jamieson, D. (2012) USDA poultry plant proposal could allow plants to speed up processing lines, stirring concern for workers, *Huffington Post*, April 19, http://www.huffingtonpost.com/2012/04/19/usda-poultry-inspections-workers_n_1438390.html, last accessed August 8, 2012.

Jarosz, L. (2009) Energy, climate change, meat, and markets: Mapping the coordinates of the current food crisis, *Geography Compass*, 3(6), pp. 2065–2083.

John, T. and P. Eyzaguirre (2007) Biofortification, biodiversity and diet: A search for complementary applications against poverty and malnutrition, *Food Policy*, 32, pp. 1–24.

Jones, T. (2005) How much goes where? The corner on food loss, *BioCycle*, July 2–3.

Kasser, T. (2002) *The High Price of Materialism*. Cambridge, MA: MIT Press.

Key, N. and M. Roberts (2007) Commodity payments, farm business survival and farm size growth, Economic Research Report No. ERR-51, Economic Research Service, USDA, Washington, DC, http://www.ers.usda.gov/Publications/ERR51/ERR51ref.pdf, last accessed June 22, 2012.

Khan, S. and M. Hanjra (2009) Footprints of water and energy inputs in food production–global perspectives, *Food Policy*, 34, pp. 130–140.

Knight, K. and E. Rosa (2011) The environmental efficiency of well-being: A cross-national analysis, *Social Science Research*, 40, pp. 931–949.

Kulkarni, S., A. Levin-Rector, M. Ezzati, and C. Murray (2011) Falling behind: Life expectancy in US counties from 2000 to 2007 in an international context, *Population Health Metrics*, 9(1), pp. 1–12.

Kumar, K., S. Gupta, S. Baidoo, Y. Chander, and C. Rosen (2005) Antibiotic uptake by plants from soil fertilized with animal manure, *Journal of Environmental Quality*, 34, pp. 2082–2085.

Land, T. and M. Heasman (2004) *Food Wars: The Global Battle for Mouths, Minds, and Markets*. London: Earthscan.

Lang, T., D. Barling, and M. Caraher (2009) *Food Policy: Integrating Health, Policy, and Society*. New York: Oxford University Press.

Lappe, F. and J. Collins (1986) *World Hunger: Twelve Myths*. New York: Grove Weidenfeld, a Food First Book.

Larson, B., M. Fox, S. Rosen, M. Bii, C. Sigei, D. Shaffer, F. Sawe, M. Wasunna, and J. Simon (2008) Early effects of antiretroviral therapy on work performance: Preliminary results from a cohort study of Kenyan agricultural workers, *AIDS*, 22, pp. 421–425.

La Via Campesina (1996) Food sovereignty: A future without hunger, http://www.voiceoftheturtle.org/library/1996%20Declaration%20of%20Food%20Sovereignty.pdf, last accessed October 22, 2012.

Lawrence, G. and P. McMichael (2012) The question of food security, *International Journal of Sociology of Agriculture and Food*, 19(2), pp. 135–142.

Leach, A. and J. Mumford (2008) Pesticide environmental accounting: A method for assessing the external costs of individual pesticide applications, *Environmental Pollution*, 151, pp. 139–147.

Lin, W., G. Price, and E. Allen (2002) Starlink: Where no Cry9C corn should have gone before, *Choices*, Winter, pp. 31–34.

Lobao, L. and C. Stofferahn (2008) The community effect of industrial farming: Social science research and challenges to corporate farming laws, *Agriculture and Human Values*, 25, pp. 219–240.

Maillot, M., N. Darmon, F. Vieux, and A. Drewnowski (2007) Low energy density and high nutritional quality are each associated with higher diet costs in French adults, *American Journal of Clinical Nutrition*, 86(3), pp. 690–696.

Marois, M. (2012) California, federal officials reveal water-tunnel plan, *Seattle Times*, July 25, http://seattletimes.com/html/nationworld/2018773226_watertunnel26.html?prmid=head_main, last accessed July 26, 2012.

Marsh, J. and G. Brester (2004) Wholesale-retail marketing margins behavior in the beef and pork industries, *Journal of Agricultural and Resource Economics*, 29(1), pp. 45–64.

McDonald's (2012) McDonald's Annual Report, 2011, http://www.aboutmcdonalds.com/content/dam/AboutMcDonalds/Investors/Investors%202012/2011%20Annual%20Report%20Final.pdf, last accessed October 23, 2012.

McKeene, H.A. (1911) *Year Book 1911*, Illinois Farmers' Institute, Department of Household Science, Springfield: Illinois State Journal Co., State Printers.

McMichael, P. (2006) Reframing development: Global peasant movements and the new agrarian question, *Canadian Journal of Development Studies*, 27(4), pp. 471–483.

Medez, A. and B. Popkin (2004) Globalization, urbanization, and nutritional change in the developing world, *Journal of Agricultural and Development Economics*, 1(2), pp. 220–241.

Miller, R., J. Webster, and S. Mariger (2004) Nonfatal injury rates of Utah agricultural producers, *Journal of Agricultural Safety and Health*, 10, pp. 285–293.

Mintz, S. (1985) *Sweetness and Power.* New York: Elisabeth Sifton Books.

Mishan, E. (1967) *The Costs of Economic Growth.* Harmondsworth: Penguin.

Mitloehner, F. and M. Calvo (2008) Worker health and safety in concentrated animal feeding operations, *Journal of Agricultural Safety and Health*, 14(2), pp. 163–187.

Mitloehner, F. and M. Schenker (2007) Environmental exposure and health effects from concentrated animal feeding operations, *Epidemiology*, 18(3), pp. 309–311.

Monivais, P., J. Mclain, and A. Drewnowski (2010) The rising disparity in the price of healthful foods: 2004–2008, *Food Policy*, 35(6), pp. 514–520.

Monteverde, M., K. Noronha, A. Palloni, and B. Novak (2010) Obesity and excess mortality among the elderly in the United States and Mexico, *Demography*, 47(1), pp. 79–96.

Mooney, P. and S. Hunt (2009) Food security: The elaboration of contested claims to a consensus frame, *Rural Sociology*, 74(4), pp. 469–497.

Morton, L., E. Bitto, M. Oakland, and M. Sand (2005) Solving the problems of Iowa food deserts: Food insecurity and civic structure, *Rural Sociology*, 70, pp. 94–112.

Moustier, P., P. Tam, D. Anh, V. Binh, and N. Loc (2010) The role of farmer organizations in supplying supermarkets with quality food in Vietnam, *Food Policy*, 35, pp. 69–78.

Mukherji, B. and B. Pattanayak (2011) New Delhi starts drive to root out hunger, *Wall Street Journal*, June 8, http://online.wsj.com/article/SB1000 1424052702304259304576372813010336844.html, last accessed July 2, 2012.

Murgai, R., M. Ali, and D. Byerlee (2001) Productivity growth and sustainability in post green-revolution agriculture: The case of Indian and Pakistani punjabs, *World Bank Research Observer*, 16(2), pp. 199–218.

Myers, N. and J. Kent (2001) *Perverse Subsidies: How Tax Dollars Can Undercut the Environment and Economy*, Washington, DC: Island Press.

Nazarea, Virginia (1998) *Cultural Memory and Biodiversity.* Tucson: University of Arizona Press.

Nazarea, Virginia (2005) *Heirloom Seeds and Their Keepers: Marginality and Memory in the Conservation of Biological Diversity.* Tucson: University of Arizona Press.

Negin, J., R. Remans, S. Karuti, and J. Fanzo (2009) Integrating a broader notion of food security and gender empowerment into the African green revolution, *Food Security*, 1, pp. 351–360.

Nestle, M. (2000) Soft drink "pouring rights": Marketing empty calories, *Public Health Reports*, 115, pp. 308–319.

Nestle, M. (2007) *Food Politics: How the Food Industry Influences Nutrition and Health*. Berkeley: University of California Press.

New Economics Foundation (2009) The Un-Happy Planet Index 2.0, http://www.happyplanetindex.org/public-data/files/happy-planet-index-2-0.pdf, last accessed April 22, 2012.

Northridge, M., E. Sclar, and P. Biswas (2003) Sorting out the connections between the built environment and health: A conceptual framework for navigating pathways and planning healthy cities, *Journal of Urban Health*, 80(4), pp. 556–568.

OECD and FAO (2012) *OECD–FAO Agricultural Outlook, 2012–2021*, Rome: FAO.

Ogino, A., H. Orito, K. Shimada, and H. Hirooka (2007) Evaluating environmental impacts of the Japanese beef cow–calf system by the life cycle assessment method, *Animal Science Journal*, 78, pp. 424–432.

Ohio State Horticultural Society (1921) *Fifty-fourth Annual Meeting of the Ohio State Horticultural Society*, Ohio State Horticultural Society, Columbus, OH: The F.J. Heer Printing Company.

OzFoodNet (2010) Food surveillance, *Food Surveillance Australia and New Zealand*, Autumn, http://www.foodstandards.gov.au/_srcfiles/Autumn%20FS%20News1.pdf, last accessed July 10, 2012.

Paarlberg, R. (2010) *Food Politics: What Everyone Needs to Know*. New York: Oxford University Press.

Pan, Xiaoqun, Cuilin Zhang, and Zumin Shi (2011) Soft drink and sweet food consumption and suicidal behaviours among Chinese adolescents, *Acta Paediatrica*, 100(11), pp. e215–e222.

Patnaik, U. (2009) Origins of the food crisis in India and developing countries, *Monthly Review*, July/August, https://www.monthlyreview.org/090727patnaik.php, last accessed October 21, 2012.

Pérez-Cueto, F., A. Bayá Botti, and W. Verbeke (2009) Prevalence of overweight in Bolivia: Data on women and adolescents, *Obesity Reviews*, 10(4), pp. 373–377.

Perfecto, I., J. Vandermeer, and A. Wright (2009) *Nature's Matrix: Linking Agriculture, Conservation and Food Sovereignty*. New York: Routledge.

Peterson, E.W. (2009) *A Billion Dollars a Day: The Economics and Politics of Agricultural Subsidies*. Malden, MA: Wiley-Blackwell.

Peterson, Roseann, Shawn Latendresse, Lindsay Bartholome, Cortney Warren, and Nancy Raymond (2012) Binge eating disorder mediates links between symptoms of depression, anxiety, and caloric intake in overweight and obese women, *Journal of Obesity*, Article ID 407103, http://www.hindawi.com/journals/jobes/2012/407103/, last accessed October 23, 2012.

Philpott, T. (2010) The fast-food industry's $4.2 billion marketing blitz, *Grist*, November 2, http://grist.org/article/food-2010–11–09-the-fast-food-industrys-4–2-billion-marketing-blitz/, last accessed July 16, 2012.

Pimentel, D. (2005) Environmental and economic costs of the application of pesticides primarily in the United States, *Environment, Development and Sustainability*, 7, pp. 229–252.

Pimentel, D. (2006) Impacts of organic farming on the efficiency of energy use in agriculture: An organic center state of science review, The Organic Center, Boulder, CO, August, http://organic.insightd.net/reportfiles/ENERGY_SSR.pdf, last accessed June 27, 2012.

Pimentel, D., P. Hepperly, J. Hanson, R. Seidel, and D. Douds (2005) Environmental, energetic, and economic comparisons of organic and conventional farming systems, *Bioscience*, 55(7), pp. 573–582.

Pimentel, D., J. Houser, E. Preiss, O. White, H. Fang, L. Mesnick, T. Barsky, S. Tariche, J. Schreck, and S. Alpert (1997) Water resources: Agriculture, the environment and society, *BioScience*, 47, pp. 97–106.

Pimentel, D., L.E. Hurd, A.C. Bellotti, M.J. Forster, I.N. Oka, O.D. Sholes, and R.J. Whitman (1973) Food production and the energy crisis, *Science*, 182(4111), pp. 443–449.

Planet retail (nd) Global food retail figures for 2011, Planet Retail, London, available online: http://www.planetretail.net (last accessed January 23, 2012).

Plummer, C. and S. Makki (2002) French fries driving globalization of frozen potato industry, *Agricultural Outlook*, 295, pp. 8–11.

Portney, K. (2003) *Taking Sustainable Cities Seriously: Economic Development, the Environment, and Quality of Life in American Cities.* Cambridge, MA: MIT Press.

Powell, L., S. Slater, D. Mirtcheva, Y. Bao, and F. Chaloupka (2007) Foodstore availability and neighborhood characteristics in the United States, *Preventive Medicine*, 44, pp. 189–195.

Pretty, J., A. Ball, T. Lang, and J. Morison (2005) Farm costs and food miles: An assessment of the full cost of the UK weekly food basket, *Food Policy*, 30, pp. 1–19.

Putman, J., J. Allshouse, and L. Kantor (2002) US per capita food supply trends, *Food Review*, 25(3), pp. 2–15.

Rayner, G., C. Hawkes, T. Lang, and W. Bello (2007) Trade liberalization and the diet transition: A public health response, *Health Promotion International*, 21(S1), pp. 64–74.

Reardon, T., C. Timmer, C. Barrett, and J. Berdegue (2003) The rise of supermarkets in Africa, Asia, and Latin America, *American Journal of Agricultural Economics*, 85(5), pp. 1140–1146.

Richards, T. and Pofahl, G. (2010) Pricing power by supermarket retailers: A ghost in the machine?, *Choices*, 25(2), http://www.choicesmagazine. org/magazine/print.php?article=126, last accessed May 21, 2012.

Rivera, J., S. Barquera, T. Gonzalez-Cossio, G. Olaiz, and J. Sepulveda (2004) Nutrition transition in Mexico and in other Latin American countries, *Nutrition Reviews*, 62, pp. S149–S157.

Roberts, P. (2008) *The End of Food*. New York: Houghton Mifflin.

Romero, Simon and Sara Shahriari (2011) A food's global success creates a quandary at home, *New York Times*, March 20, http://www.nytimes. com/2011/03/20/world/americas/20bolivia.html, last accessed July 26, 2012.

Rose, D., J. Bodor, C. Swalm, J. Rice, T. Fraley, and P. Hutchinson (2009) Deserts in New Orleans? Illustrations of urban food access and implications for policy, National Poverty Center working paper, http://www.npc. umich.edu/news/events/food-access/rose_et_al.pdf, last accessed October 15, 2012.

Rose, D. and R. Richards (2004) Food store access and household fruit and vegetable use among participants in the US Food Stamp Program, *Public Health and Nutrition*, 7, pp. 1081–1088.

Rosegrant, M., C. Ringler, and T. Zhu (2009) Water for agriculture: Maintaining food security under growing scarcity, *Annual Review of Environmental Resources*, 34, pp. 205–222.

Rosegrant, M., R. Valmonte-Santos, S. Cline, C. Ringler, and W. Li (2005) Water resources, agriculture and pasture: Implications of growing demand and increasing scarcity, in D. McGilloway (ed.) *Grassland: A Global Resource*. Netherlands: Wageningen, pp. 227–238.

Sachs, J. (1999) Food at the center of global crisis, World Food Prize, 2009, Norman E. Borlaug International Symposium, Food, Agriculture, and National Security in a Globalized World, Des Moines, IA, October 14–16, http://208.109.245.191/assets/Symposium/2009/transcripts/2009-Borlaug-Dialogue-Sachs.pdf, last accessed October 21, 2012.

Sage, C. (2011) *Environment and Food*. New York: Routledge.

Sasson, A. (2012) Food security for Africa: An urgent global challenge, *Agriculture and Food Security*, 1(2), pp. 1–16.

Schor, J. (2005) *Born to Buy*. New York: Scribner.

Scott, L., P. McGee, C. Walsh, S. Fanning, T. Sweeney, J. Blanco, M. Karczmarczyk, B. Earley, N. Leonard, and J.J. Sheridan (2009) Detection of numerous verotoxigenic E. coli serotypes, with multiple antibiotic resistance from cattle faeces and soil, *Veterinary Microbiology*, 134(3–4), pp. 288–293.

Scrinis, G. (2008) On the ideology of nutritionism, *Gastronomica*, 8(1), pp. 38–48

Settle, R. (1983) Evaluating the economic benefits of pesticide usage, *Agriculture, Ecosystems and the Environment*, 9(2), pp. 173–185.

Shariff, Z. and G. Khor (2005) Obesity and household food insecurity: Evidence from a sample of rural households in Malaysia, *European Journal of Clinical Nutrition*, 59, pp. 1049–1058.

Shaw, D.J. (2007) *World Food Security: A History since 1945*. New York: Palgrave.

Shaw, H. (2006) Food deserts: Towards the development of a classification, *Geografiska annaler*, 88(2), pp. 231–247.

Shimp, T. (2009) *Advertising Promotion and Other Aspects of Integrated Marketing*, Mason, OH: South-Western Cengage Learning.

Smith, G. (2012) Agribusiness in the US industry market research report now available from IBIS World, July 9, http://www.prweb.com/releases/2012/3/prweb9265884.htm, last accessed July 9, 2012.

Smith, M., J. Pointing, and S. Maxwell (1992) *Household Food Security, Concepts and Definitions: An Annotated Bibliography*, Development Bibliography No. 8. Brighton: Institute of Development Studies, University of Sussex.

Smith, P., D. Martino, Z. Cai, D. Gwary, H. Janzen, P. Kumar, B. McCarl, S. Ogle, F. O'Mara, C. Rice, B. Scholes, and O. Sirotenko (2007) Agriculture, in B. Metz, O.R. Davidson, P.R. Bosch, R. Dave, and L.A. Meyer (eds) *Climate Change 2007: Mitigation. Contribution of Working Group III to the Fourth Assessment Report of the Intergovernmental Panel on Climate Change*. Cambridge and New York: Cambridge University Press, http://www.ipcc.ch/publications_and_data/ar4/wg3/en/ch8.html, last accessed June 22, 2012.

Steinbeck, J. (2006 [1939]) *The Grapes of Wrath*. New York: Penguin.

Stofferahn, C. (2006) Industrialized farming and its relationship to community well-being: An update of a 2000 report by Linda Lobao, paper prepared for the State of North Dakota, Office of the Attorney General, September.

Stringer, C. and R. Le Heron (eds) (2008) *Agri-Food Commodity Chains and Globalizing Networks*. Burlington, VT: Ashgate.

Stuart, T. (2009) *Waste: Uncovering the Global Food Scandal*. New York: Norton.

Sutherland, R. (2010) We can't run away from the ethical debates in marketing, *Market Leader*, January, http://www.marketing-society.org.uk/SiteCollectionDocuments/knowledge-zone/market-leader/january-2010.pdf, last accessed April 8, 2012.

Swinburn, B. and G. Egger (2002) Preventive strategies against weight gain and obesity, *Obesity Reviews*, 3(4), pp. 289–301.

Taylor, C. (2004) *Modern Social Imaginaries*. Durham, NC: Duke University Press.

Taylor, R. and D. Domina (2010) Restoring economic health to contract poultry production, report prepared for the Joint US Department of Justice and US Department of Agriculture/GIPSA Public Workshop on Competition Issues in the Poultry Industry, May 21, Normal, AL,

http://www.dominalaw.com/ew_library_file/ Restoring%20Economic%20
Health%20to%20Contract%20Poultry%20Production.pdf, last accessed
July 24, 2012.

Thompson, E.P. (1971) The moral economy of the English crowd in the
eighteenth century, *Past and Present*, 50, pp. 76–136.

Toops, D. (2011) Food processors find public growth for private label,
Food Processing, July 18, http://www.foodprocessing.com/articles/
2011/private-label.html, last accessed July 9, 2012.

Ulyatt, M. and K. Lassey (2001) Methane emissions from pastoral systems:
The situation in New Zealand, *Latin American Association of Animal
Production*, 9(1), pp. 118–126.

Union of Concerned Scientists (2008) Preservation of Antibiotics for
Medical Treatment Act, http://www.ucsusa.org/food_and_agriculture/
solutions/wise_antibiotics/pamta.html, last accessed July 10, 2012.

United Nations (1975) Report of the World Food Conference, Rome,
November 5–16, 1974. Document E/Conf. 65/20.

United Nations (2007) Human Development Report 2006, United Nations
Development Program, New York, http://hdr.undp.org/en/media/
HDR06-complete.pdf, last accessed March 16, 2012.

USDA (2005) Dietary guidelines for Americans 2005, http://www.health.
gov/dietaryguidelines/dga2005/document/html/chapter2.htm, last accessed
July 6, 2012.

USDA (2009) Access to affordable and nutritious food: Measuring
and understanding food deserts and their consequences, report to
Congress, June, http://www.ers.usda.gov/media/242675/ap036_1_.pdf,
last accessed July 16, 2012.

USDA (2011) *International Food Security Assessment, 2011–21*,
http://www.ers.usda.gov/media/123436/gfa22.pdf, last accessed July 17,
2012.

USDA Economic Research Service (2002) The US food marketing system,
http://www.ers.usda.gov/publications/aer811/aer811.pdf, last accessed
October 15, 2012.

Vaccari, D. (2009) Phosphorus famine: The threat to our food supply,
Scientific American, June 3, pp. 54–59.

Van den Bosch, R. (1978) *The Pesticide Conspiracy*. Garden City, NY:
Doubleday.

Van Der Hoek, W., F. Konradsen, K. Athukorala, and T. Wanigadewa
(1998) Pesticide poisoning: A major health problem in Sri Lanka, *Social
Science and Medicine*, 46(4), pp. 495–504.

van der Ploeg, Jan (2008) *The New Peasantries: Struggles for Autonomy
and Sustainability in an Era of Empire and Globalization*. London:
Earthscan.

Veenhoven, R. (1996) Happy life expectancy, *Social Indicators Research*,
39(1), pp. 1–58.

Venkat, K. (2011) The climate change and economic impacts of food waste in the United States, *International Journal of Food System Dynamics*, 2(4), pp. 431–446.

Vollrath, D. (2007) Land distribution and international agricultural productivity, *American Journal of Agricultural Economics*, 89(1), pp. 202–216.

Vollrath, D. and L. Erickson (2007) Land distribution and financial system development, IMF Working Paper WP/03/83, International Monetary Fund, http://www.imf.org/external/pubs/ft/wp/2007/wp0783.pdf, last accessed June 4, 2012.

von Braun, J. (2007) The world food situation: New driving forces and required actions, Food Policy Report, December, International Food Policy Research Institute, Washington, DC, http://www.ifad.org/events/lectures/ifpri/pr18.pdf, last accessed July 9, 2012.

Walmart (2012) Walmart reports Q1 EPS of $1.09, above guidance, press release, May 17, http://media.corporate-ir.net/media_files/irol/11/112761/release/Q1FY13Release.pdf, last accessed October 21, 2012.

Wang, Y., C. Lehane, K. Ghebremeskel, and M. Crawford (2009) Modern organic and broiler chickens sold for human consumption provide more energy from fat than protein, *Public Health Nutrition*, 13(3), pp. 400–408.

Wardle, J. and M. Baranovic (2009) Is lacking of retail competition in the grocery sector a public health issue?, *Australian and New Zealand Journal of Public Health*, 33(5), pp. 477–481.

Warwick, H. (2001) Cuba's organic revolution, *Forum for Applied Research and Public Policy*, Summer, pp. 54–58.

Webb, A., A. Schiff, D. Currivan, and E. Villamor (2008) Food stamp program participation but not food insecurity is associated with higher adult BMI in Massachusetts residents living in low-income neighborhoods, *Public Health Nutrition*, 11(12), pp. 1248–1255.

Weber, C. and H.S. Matthews (2008) Food miles and the relative climate impacts of food choices in the United States, *Environmental Science and Technology*, 42(10), pp. 3508–3513.

Week, The (2011) Bolivia's quinoa quandary, March 22, http://theweek.com/article/index/213390/bolivias-quinoa-quandary, last accessed July 26, 2012.

Weinberg, Z. (1995) *No Place to Shop: The Lack of Supermarkets in Low-Income Neighborhoods*, Washington, DC: Public Voice for Food and Health Policy.

Weise, E. (2010) USA pays price for food-borne illness: $152b a year, *USA Today*, March 4, http://www.usatoday.com/news/health/2010–03–03-food-borne-illness_N.htm, last accessed July 10, 2012.

Welsh, R. and R. Graham (1999) A new paradigm for world agriculture, *Field Crops Research*, 60, pp. 1–10.

Wesseling, C., L. Castillo, and C. Elinder (1993) Pesticide poisonings in Costa Rica, *Scandinavian Journal of Work, Environment and Health*, 19(4), pp. 227–235.

Wilkinson, R. and K. Pickett (2009) *The Spirit Level: Why More Equal Societies Are Almost Always Better*. New York: Penguin.

Wilkinson, R., K. Pickett, and R. De Vogli (2010) Equality, sustainability, and quality of life, *British Medical Journal*, 341, pp. 1138–1140.

Williams, G., P. Metha, and K. Willis (2009) *Geographies of Developing Areas: The Global South in a Changing World*. New York: Routledge.

Williamson, Stephanie (2005) Breaking the barriers to IPM in Africa: Evidence from Benin, Ethiopia, Ghana, and Senegal, in Jules Petty (ed.) *The Pesticide Detox*. London: Earthscan, pp. 165–180.

Wise, T. (2010) Monopolies are killing our farms: Editorial, *East Texas Review*, April 13, http://www.ase.tufts.edu/gdae/Pubs/rp/WiseMonopolies AndFarms13Apr10.pdf, last accessed October 21, 2012.

Wise, T. (2012) Running on empty: US ethanol policies set to reach their illogical conclusion, *Triple Crisis*, July 23, http://triplecrisis.com/running-on-empty-u-s-ethanol-policies-set-to-reach-their-illogical-conclusion/, last accessed July 26, 2012.

Wittman, H., A. Desmarais, and N. Wiebe (2010) *Food Sovereignty: Reconnecting Food, Nature and Community*. Oakland, CA: Food First Books.

Woods, J., A. Williams, J. Hughes, M. Black, and R. Murphy (2010) Energy and the food system, *Philosophical Transactions of the Royal Society B Biological Sciences*, 365(1554), pp. 2991–3006.

World Bank (2002) *Global Economic Prospects and the Developing Countries: Making Trade Work for the World's Poor*, Washington, DC: World Bank.

World Bank (2009) *Gender in Agriculture Sourcebook*, http://siteresources.worldbank.org/INTGENAGRLIVSOUBOOK/Resources/CompleteBook.pdf, last accessed July 15, 2012

WTO (2002) Trade liberalization and food security, speech by Miguel Rodríguez Mendoza, Deputy Director-General of the WTO to the World Food Summit, Rome, June 11.

Xin, Z., W. Kaihao, and C. Anqi (2012) Waste not, want not, *China Daily*, http://www.chinadaily.com.cn/cndy/2012–01/19/content_14472383.htm, last accessed July 2, 2012.

Zenk, S., A. Schulz, B. Israel, S. James, S. Bao, and M. Wilson (2005) Neighborhood racial composition, neighborhood poverty, and the spatial accessibility of supermarkets in metropolitan Detroit, *American Journal of Public Health*, 95(4), pp. 660–667.

Zepeda, E., T. Wise, and K. Gallagher (2008) Rethinking trade policy for development: Lessons from Mexico under NAFTA, policy outlook,

Carnegie Endowment for International Peace, Washington, DC, http://www.carnegieendowment.org/files/nafta_trade_development.pdf, last accessed July 25, 2012.

Zerbe, N. (2009) Setting the global dinner table: Exploring the limits of the marketization of food security, in J. Clapp and M. Cohen (eds) *The Global Food Crisis: Governance Challenges and Opportunities.* Waterloo, Ontario: Wilfrid University Laurier Press, pp. 161–175.

Ziegler, M. (1922) The history of the calorie in nutrition, *Scientific Monthly*, 15(6), pp. 520–526.

Zimmerman, F. (2011) Using marketing muscle to sell fat: The rise of obesity in the modern economy, *Annual Review of Public Health*, 32, pp. 285–306.

Index

Printed in Great Britain
by Amazon